SPIRIT IN STONE
The Spirituality of the Greater Churches

Spirit in Stone
The Spirituality of the Greater Churches

Roger Bellamy

Pentland Books
Durham · Edinburgh · Oxford

© Roger Bellamy 2001

First published in 2001 by
Pentland Books
1 Hutton Close
South Church
Bishop Auckland
Durham

British Library Cataloguing in Publication Data.
A catalogue record for this book is available
from the British Library.

ISBN 1 85821 853 5

Typeset by George Wishart & Associates, Whitley Bay.
Printed and bound by Antony Rowe Ltd., Chippenham.

For Tom to go with all the postcards

Contents

Introduction

On a bookshelf in my childhood home was a slim, paper-covered book on English cathedrals. It had black and white drawings, some of which I can still see in my mind's eye: the great circular pillars at Gloucester, the deeply carved screen at Exeter, the carved leaves of the Chapter House at Southwell. From my first glimpse of those pages I was hooked, but it was years before I was able to see most of these churches. I had to be content with what was more immediately around. Our village had a large perpendicular church with wild, grotesque carvings jostling with beatific ones in the oak roofs. Winged waterbirds of the Fenland and angels with symbols of the Passion both seemed about to take wing. It was one of the several churches which had inspired D.L. Sayers' *The Nine Tailors*.

Often we stayed with my grandparents in a small nearby town. Their church, high, to my child's mind, on a cliff, was small and dark inside, full of mystery. Its reddy brown carr stone making a strong contrast with the grey Barnack of my own village church. These were the first places in which I learnt to worship. I couldn't have put it into words then and probably can't now, but I sensed that these stones, glass, timber, lead were more than just the elements which made a building like the bricks, mortar and slates of our house or the red-brick and tile of the school.

Not far away were two other important places: King's Chapel in Cambridge and Ely Cathedral. Vastly different they are. Now I recognize King's as superb, delicate but also deeply proud, rather fussy and too gorgeous. Too much of Henry VIII. It's spirituality for me is too far invaded by human pride.

Ely on its remote hill speaks in whispers, in deep tête-à-tête conversations, intimate yet so public, private and homely as well as grand. The stone, seen often from the railway from Lynn to Liverpool Street, changes constantly from a dull sullen grey to the brightest silver. The octagon glimpsed with eyes searching the flat landscape, knowing the very moment when it would appear, but always wondering, hoping, praying that it would still be there. And, yes, every time the miracle. It is there, delicate, held aloft, floating against the Fenland sky.

Of these places was born my love of churches: the small and the great. But for many years now it has been the greater ones that I have found echoing my own spirituality. Just as Bach suites do, and Beethoven symphonies. There is some kind of match between what is happening in me and it is this that I want to explore in this book.

The opportunity came with a Sabbatical in 1998. So I am grateful to the Diocese of Sheffield, the people of my parish and my assistant, Fr Philip Arnold, for making those three months available to me.

I write as a Christian within the high Anglican tradition and I suppose in some ways for those who share my beliefs, but not only for them. I believe that the spirituality of these great churches is deeply human, and that is perhaps why so many non- or irregular worshippers visit them just as many non-churchgoers listen to the Missa Solemnis or the St Matthew Passion, or look at great religious paintings. But that merely human element can be the way into something deeper, something invisible that transcends the visible. For those who share my faith I want to unlock the treasures, the deeper ways of the Spirit that these stones were built to celebrate.

I will tell the Jewish-Christian story. There will be dates and architectural history, but also theology and prayer. It is not a guide book. If it succeeds in its purpose it will be a guide, but one that will lead your heart and soul as much as your feet and eyes.

Before we go any further I must define what I mean by 'greater' church. They have many features but just a few mark them off from 'lesser' churches. It isn't necessarily a matter of size or even scale although they do tend to be large. A complexity of design is nearly always apparent: an extravagance expressed in height and hidden interior spaces. Height is achieved by making the principal spaces three storeyed. That is to say the elevation has three levels. The aisles are actually two storeyed although they appear to be only one. The arcade of pillars and arches divides the main areas from the aisles and the aisles are ceiled with a stone vault. Above this, and below the sloping roof, is the aisle and the nave's second storey. It is called the gallery and originally, at least, had no windows, but openings of a single arch with a number of sub-arches beneath it to form the second level of the elevation. Sometimes it has three openings and thus was called triforium, but it is silly to use that term when there are two or four or more arches, so I use gallery throughout.

The third storey is the clerestory, rising above the gallery, and having the windows which light the main space. From within this level and sometimes continuing from below, are the ribs for the high vault. Not all greater churches have a high vault. Ely and Peterborough, for example, have panelled ceilings, and more rarely there are open timber roofs. Above the vault and below the steeply pitched roof is another large space – the roof void. The vault acts as a firebreak and if the roof was to be well drained then the high pitch made this 'wasted' space inevitable.

Much of this space has no liturgical use, but practical galleries, passageways at clerestory level, roof voids together with spiral staircases make the care and maintenance of the building easier. It is almost as if there is a permanent internal scaffold in place. Another practical aspect of the gallery is that the stone vault adds to the buttressing of the nave walls, countering the outward thrust of the high vaults.

Another complex feature is the division of the main areas. Greater churches are not one or even two spaces, but many. The areas have different functions and may be divided off by walls, solid screens, even flights of stairs. This multi-form space grew out of building a series of smaller buildings, and then gradually transforming them into one. The best place for observing this process is in Canterbury. Not at the cathedral but at the nearby St Augustine's Abbey. You can read the details in Glyn Coppack's Abbeys and Priories.[1] The plan reproduced here in simplified form shows the original church. This was then extended westwards. To the east and at some distance was a further church, and later another was built to the west. In the eleventh century the original church and the eastern one were linked by Abbot Wulfric but his work was never completed and overtaken in scale by Abbot Scotland rebuilding the whole complex from 1073.

All the medieval cathedrals were built as greater churches and most of the rest were built as abbeys or priories although their present status may well be parochial. Interestingly, with the exception of Romsey Abbey, they were all built for men's communities. A few greater churches were built for colleges of priests and some of these are rather borderline between greater and lesser. Manchester Cathedral is such an example.

If in doubt look for four main features: thee-storeyed elevation, stone vaults, multi-spaced and with a central tower. There is also an air of architectural quality: fine stone, good carving, rich furnishings. They continue to attract greater resources both financial and human, and one hopes, therefore, to find a deeper spirituality.

And now before we come to the churches themselves we must explore what we mean by spirituality.

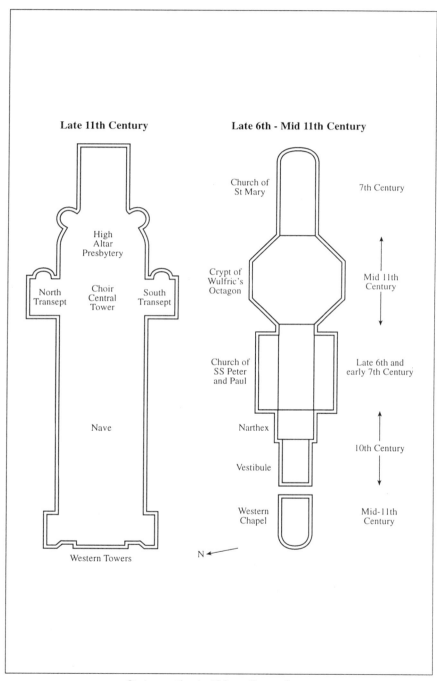

Late 11th Century

Late 6th - Mid 11th Century

High Altar Presbytery

North Transept

Choir Central Tower

South Transept

Nave

Western Towers

Church of St Mary

Crypt of Wulfric's Octagon

Church of SS Peter and Paul

Narthex

Vestibule

Western Chapel

7th Century

Mid 11th Century

Late 6th and early 7th Century

10th Century

Mid-11th Century

N

St Augustine's Abbey, Canterbury.

xii

The unique thirteenth century Lantern tower seems to hang in space at the centre of Ely Cathedral: an example of daring building.

The late medieval east window of York Minster.

The late medieval east window of York Minster.

The west window of Chester Cathedral.

The recently installed window at Sherborne Abbey making a theological statement about the lives of Mary and Christ.

CHAPTER I

Spirituality

In a book about buildings and spirituality perhaps we had better start with spirituality for it is a much used but little understood word. Spirituality is the central nerve of the Christian life, our life in the Spirit. It asserts that we are spiritual. Not just body and mind, but having a deep, inner life. Hebrew and Greek have only a single word each for spirit, breath and wind, which means that our use of such words must have deep layers of meaning. The words resonate profoundly. The spiritual nature of human beings means that we have within us the ability to transcend ourselves and to reach out to a far greater reality beyond ourselves. Robert Waddington wrote of church schools as beacons that signal transcendence.[1] That is true not only of Christian schools as a community but also of churches, both the people and the buildings, and of all of us humans. Not everyone sees themselves as having transcendency but I think it is in the nature of being human. Christians are, however, committed to that belief. We are, as St John Chrysostom insists, 'people who believe in more than we can see'. 'Visible and invisible', as the Nicene Creed puts it. (The translation in common use of 'seen and unseen', does not mean the same. The kettle in my kitchen is currently unseen because I am in a different room, but will be seen if I go to make a cup of tea. Whereas the truly invisible remains invisible.) We recognize ourselves as showing both the visible and the invisible. Body and spirit: bodies inbreathed by God. It is something of the Christian mission to help others to find and to heed the spirit deep within.

Look at the second story of creation in Genesis 2. We see that God forms a man out of the dust (Adam) of the earth, and then breathes into him the breath of life (Gen 2.7). Our breath is a metaphor of our invisible, spiritual nature. In not only recognizing this about ourselves, but by seeking to nourish this inbreathing, is our spirituality. We can transcend ourselves. All sorts of possibilities open up. The past is no longer to determine the future. There is room for genuine creativity, and in his transcendence man is free to hear the call of the transcendent God. God is seeking us and in our depths we are searching for Him although we may not be able to name Him.

1

It is this that so many non-Christians recognize in the spiritual world, and not only Muslims and Jews but many humanists. Life in the Spirit is a life aware of the divine, and aware of our brothers and sisters. A life of communion, which is signalled by our little, incomplete, fragmentary communions but which will find its transcendent meaning in that great communion of heaven: 'angels and archangels and all the company of heaven', as we sing in the Mass and will sing, around God's throne where the unity of the cosmos will be manifested. The vision of the New Jerusalem in Revelation is pointing to that with its multiples of twelve, representing the twelve tribes of Israel, and the apostles of Christ as the foundation stones of the new Israel. The city is 12 furlongs square and its wall 144 cubits high. The fullness, the maturity to which God calls us, is the stature of Christ in whom the unity of all creation is to be found.

The life of the Holy Trinity, to whom most of the greater churches are dedicated, is the source of our life. We are caught up into the Trinity Himself. For example, prayer is to the Father, through the Son and by the power of the Holy Spirit. The Holy Spirit dwells in our hearts and by His power Christ comes to us in the Mass.

The greater churches draw us to reflect on the God in whose honour they were built, and on His purposes for us and our own spiritual journey.

St Benedict, whose followers built a number of the greater churches, writes in the Prologue of his Rule about the spiritual life.

> If we want to escape the pains of hell and attain everlasting life, then, while there is still time, while we are in the body and can still do all these things by the light of this life, we must make haste to do at once what will profit us for all eternity. We must, therefore, establish a school for the Lord's service. In setting out its regulations, we hope to impose nothing harsh or burdensome . . . As we advance in monastic life and in faith, our hearts will grow, and we shall run with an inexpressible sweetness of love along the way of God's command-ments . . . We shall share by patience in the sufferings of Christ, that we may deserve to share also in his kingdom.[2]

That 'school of the Lord's service' is one community in which men and women may run towards God's kingdom. Each of us needs to find the 'school' that God wills for us. In whose company, in what ways, along which path are we to run towards God? For most the school will not be one place but many. It will have stable elements, the things which root us and nourish us, but the curriculum (to continue

Benedict's image) will have many aspects. The greater churches visited for worship, for times of silence, on pilgrimage, to pray at a shrine, for great services, or just to wander around in, to linger and stand and gaze, may for many be part of that schooling.

We are learning to draw on a wide menu of spiritual resources. The Rule of St Benedict, Celtic spirituality, Ignatian, the riches of liturgical renewal, for example, but there are a great many more. I think the greater churches are also a spiritual resource, not only in the ways they are used, but simply in themselves, if we learn how to listen to them.

But this 'school' must create in us a passion for life, a passion for justice, for mercy and peace. 'Send us out,' we pray. 'Go', commands the priest, and that we must do. Spirituality is not to be encompassed in churchy things, however holy. St Benedict's monastery was a complete world with an holistic view of life: body and spirit, mind and heart. He writes about prayer, but also about work, about sleeping arrangements and food, about ways of government. And in this, of course, he is echoing the Gospel. Jesus' Good News confronts us with the demands of justice, of mercy, forgiveness. Love of God but, hand in hand, indivisibly, love of neighbour. That loving is to be done where we are, whether in cloister, school, parish, office, factory, village, city estate, hospital, shopping mall. The people who are where we are are our neighbours whom we are to love and serve.

If greater churches draw us away from humanity, from suffering, from the search for justice, then they are no longer houses of the Spirit but only places of some comfortable aesthetic. The Gospel drags us into the world with Jesus, in caring for the sick, the poor, the disadvantaged, and sometimes we find ourselves enduring these things with Christ.

I do not see a conflict. The image and symbols of heaven point us back again and again to the world, to rejoice in its beauty and to delight in its glories, but to be with Christ in the hungry, the homeless, the naked, the sick, the imprisoned and to allow the vision of glory to give us a vision of our world as it can be, transfigured by light and love. 'Thy will be done on earth, as it is in heaven,' we pray.

The sources of our spirituality are not only our prayer, worship, the 'things of the Spirit', but everything. All is grist to the mill: our social life, politics, sexuality, work, recreation, family: everything belongs to be reflected on, even our sin. So although this book begins with these great churches it constantly points us toward God and to every aspect of life without exception. 'Nothing human is alien to man' – and we might add to Terence's dictum, nor anything divine.

For some people the greater church is a place of regular worship, either because you are a member of the foundation or because you choose to worship there. For others they may be places of worship for a period of life, but one which holds treasured memories. I know for some they are places of incomprehension and unlovingness. For most they are places to visit. I am certain they are a spiritual resource but one which their custodians must guard carefully.

In my preparations for writing this I visited most of the greater churches. I arrived as it were at random. I did not find out what might be happening, and I did encounter quite a lot of activities. But the one incident I want to relate at this point was in Salisbury. It was a spring day when the rain fell torrentially. I made my way, trying to keep dry under an umbrella, across the Close, past the scaffold-shrouded west front and to the cloister entrance where I knew visitors enter. In the dry, I paid my money. The ticket speaks of a donation. I'm not sure that is the right word, although I happily paid the money. I hadn't got as far as the nave when the noise hit me. The front half of the nave was filled with some 150 schoolgirls, aged, I guess, 9-13. They were there preparing for some important school anniversary commemoration. I was in the cathedral itself for about forty-five minutes. The only time this loud noise – for it wasn't hushed whispers, but conversation and laughter which filled the cathedral as much as the organ playing would have done – stopped was when a priest briefly led some prayers. In addition to the children there were several parties of people being guided around the building, the guides trying to make themselves heard and so with raised voices too. The visitors have come to see the architecture but mightn't they be more encouraged to see 'cathedral' rather than wonderful medieval architecture? Cameras flash constantly and at numerous points around the building are encouragements to part with money: a stall for your family name's history, for example. That was in the Cloister. I ventured to the Chapter House, but that too was full of noise. I write of Salisbury but it could have been many other cathedrals. The problem is created by their 'success' and deans and chapters need the money these folk bring, but is this what these places are for? I am not suggesting that no other activity but worship should take place in them, although Benedict does say that the Oratory should always be silent, but in the noise, in the guides' voices, the visitor loses the atmosphere, the purpose of the building. Yes, they are ancient monuments, but that is very much secondary. Chapels set aside for private prayer are good, but they also send the wrong signal to the visitor. This, they say, is the place to pray, the main building isn't for prayer.

The authorities need to decide whether their churches are truly churches all the time, with occasional use that doesn't detract from that purpose, or whether they are only truly churches when services are taking place. Meanwhile I encourage you not to go to York or Salisbury. Get off the beaten track. Go to Chichester, or Southwell, Peterborough or Tewskesbury. The numbers of visitors isn't really the issue. It is what they come for and whether, when there are guided tours, noisy children, heritage displays and so on, the visitor is being cheated. He may come out of the rain, or just because it's there to visit, but he ought to go away taking something of the Spirit with him. And he had no chance of doing that, that particular morning in Salisbury.

The majority of our greater churches were built in an age of faith when Europe was Christendom, but now we live in an age of doubt and fear, of technological revolutions, or an empty materialism for the rich and desperate poverty for millions in Africa, South America and Asia. The Church in England, a minority, despite the claim by most people to believe in God, remains engaged with society. There are many similarities with the age of Benedict. Society's institutions are in decline and in need of reformation. The old channels have been silted up and the water is largely stagnant. People live with expectations attenuated. The problems of everyday – economic, crime, drugs, education, the lack of money for so many good causes despite high taxation – these problems overwhelm many people. Their sights are limited, to the material, the urgent, no time or even less reason, to stand and to stare, when time is abundant. Thomas Maude, the stonemason, says that to stand and stare has always been one of his pastimes. 'It doesn't cost anything and indeed the longer one lingers and dreams, the richer one becomes.'[3] That is to look at life contemplatively. Bishop Holloway describes that kind of looking as 'passionate, attached, at one with what one beholds, seeing with the subjectivity and involvement of the lover watching the beloved. Everything is enlarged and widened and loaded with significance.'[4] Worship and prayer are about play and wholeness and remembrance. That is a contemplative thing: seeing myself in these real terms, in the context, as it were, of God and neighbour. Cathedrals draw us into that reality for without God they would not exist and they do speak of God as He reveals Himself in Scripture and in Christian lives. Although those things in their turn help to create them, the vision came first. Often misunderstood, as Golding's Dean is misunderstood, and for different reasons by Pangall, the verger, Roger, the mason and Anselm, the sacrist. But the vision has power.

In the cathedral we are drawn into a community. One can't ignore the neighbour, and the liturgy, always a communal thing, pulls us into the divine life, but equally firmly shoves us out into the injustices of the world. Marketplace and desert is how Cardinal Hume described that double edge. The Jews knew that of old. The Tabernacle focussing their relationship with God in worship contained the Commandments which forged their ethics and morality: worship and mercy and justice are bound together.

Eric Gill spoke of his strange life (full of contradictions as it was) as the attempt to make a cell of good living in the chaos of the world. Knowing what we do about him it would seem to most that chaos invaded his cell, but the idea is still valid and that is what the Church seeks to be: cells of good living in the chaos of the world. But the degree to which we are engaged with the chaos is also important. The edges between cell and chaos are never clear. Indeed I do not believe they can be. The cells are not so convinced of their own absolute rightness that they do not listen to the world. Dialogue remains vital. Some Christians want a hard distinction between Church and world, but if that is ever appropriate it can't be so in the context of these greater churches. The monastery of St Benedict, despite its enclosure, remains open to the world. The Regular Canons deliberately set themselves towards the needs of people and the medieval prebendal cathedrals thronged with humanity. The Cistercian communities were largely self-contained – cells of good living; but as any contemplative monk will relate, living an enclosed life brings you closer to humanity rather than farther away.

Indeed for most of us on the journey towards God, there is the cell and chaos within us. We bring the chaos into the Church with us. Each place, each group of people, does its bit. The greater churches may be flagships, but also points of contact, where the Church can learn to understand something more of the chaos and other people's view of what we Christians call chaos, for not all agree with our viewpoint, and my chaos may be order to others. Great churches are also places in which to tell others of what lies at the heart of the hope that is within us. Boundary people having deep roots in God but still very open to the chaos and having empathy and even sympathy with it are necessary in these liminal places.

Rose Tremain writes: 'a place where extraordinary things could happen in it like Wembley Arena or the Cheddar Gorge, say things he'd never said before and listen to the echo of them'.[5] Isn't there something of that in these churches? A sense of expectancy of possibilities, of daring?

'A place for daring: as high as you dare.'

'And what is the good of a small dare, Roger? My dares are big ones.'

'Well?'

'Four hundred feet of dare. I haven't convinced you then?'[6]

Too many people try to convince us, but we need to dare, and the Christian faith is a place in which we can make big dares – for God made a great dare in making us, and by the greatest dare of all, raised Christ, and us, to new life. We dare to join the cell of good living. We dare to remain engaged with the chaos. We dare to admit that we are not entirely void of the chaos ourselves, but we are on the way, and we dare to keep going.

These churches especially are places where the dare of worship, the dare of mission are to the fore, echoing the architectural dare which created them, the dare shooting up out of a deep, spiritual vision. Christianity is the belief in the art of the possible, of potential, of capabilities, of always moving on, firmly rooted, but engaged with the God who comes to us from the future as well as being the source of all, and our present companion.

Cathedrals and abbeys point us back to our roots – we remember. They celebrate our present experience and they challenge us with the unlimitable hopes for the future.

CHAPTER II

Bezalel and Aholiab

These are not the best-known names of the Old Testament. They come in Exodus, in the account about making the Ark of the Tabernacle. This box, containing the stone tablets of the Law, was to be the central icon of the Jewish faith. Bezalel, Moses tells the people, has been filled by God 'with the divine spirit, making him skilful, expert in every craft and a master of design'. Their skills encompass metalwork, wood, engraving and embroidery and they were also responsible for the Tent of the Presence, so presumably able to work skins as well. In addition they were the designers of vestments. All this is to be found in Exodus 35.30ff. In other words they were the architects, designers and craftsmen of their day and their skills are attributed to the divine spirit, the divine breath, the Holy Spirit of God. This is important because it reveals that the Jews saw God at work not only in the liturgy itself but in the artefacts and 'buildings' required to carry out the liturgy. The tradition continues down the ages, and we can see the divine inspiration in masons, glass-makers, carpenters as well as painters, musicians, organ-builders: for all these are ways through which the Holy Spirit is able to address mankind.

In a lecture given in Chichester in 1954 T.S. Eliot spoke of the purpose of cathedrals as being 'the worship of God according to the rites of the Church' (p. 5).[1] That is true of all churches but the resources of greater churches are such that the foundation itself, whether that of a cathedral, or in medieval times of a monastery, can perform this yearly cycle of liturgy without the presence or involvement of a congregation. In a different way a parish church does its liturgy without outside resources, so, but much more fully, does a greater church. Of course there are many big occasions when others become an integral part of the liturgy: ordinations for example, but these are extra to the ordinary round of liturgy: the office and the Eucharist.

We may, however, as it were, eavesdrop on this liturgy. Most days a small congregation gathers for Evensong in a cathedral. Some will be kind of honorary members of the foundation by virtue of their regular attendance, others will be visitors there just for one service. Some people find the kind of worship, where perhaps apart from a hymn they are not expected to make any audible contribution, rather hard to take. But this is a liturgy which we can receive. Others say the words, sing the music, but set free from the need to do those things, we may pray at a deeper level than otherwise we might be able to reach. And this does not mean not being involved. At a concert or in the theatre we may be totally involved, caught up in the music, the drama, but we are not active in the sense of being on the platform playing an instrument or a role. The audience may seem passive, but the interior activity is just not especially visible. It becomes so, I suppose, when we sit on the edge of our seats, or in the liturgical context, our eyes are shut but we are obviously serenely at one with the worship, or even at moments when there are tears of joy. Not joining in does not mean not involved, not worshipping: rather the contrary.

The liturgy itself, but the building too, may be a source of communion with God. We can seize and use the opportunity of worship or a visit to an empty cathedral 'to catch again the breath of God'. These are words of Somerset Ward in his important 'but much neglected work, *To Jerusalem*. He was writing of devotional reading and went on to speak of the breath of God 'enclosed in human words'.[2] Well, may I just alter that to 'enclosed in human artefacts and activities'? If God's power and wisdom has been inbreathed then it is there just as much in stone and glass, in space and liturgical ordering as it is in words.

Catching the breath of God is not easy. It requires being open, prepared, expectant. Somerset Ward again: 'The inbreathing of God will not be apprehended save by those who are in a condition which it can penetrate.' Not only were Bezalel and Aholiab inbreathed by the Spirit, others had to recognize that they themselves received the in-breathing through the artists' work. It is that contemplative way of looking, the lingering, the standing and staring, looking with eyes of love, with a heart of adoration, that enables God's breath to penetrate: and isn't that love and adoration grounded in God and the magnetic effect of His beauty? I guess initially we are 'caught' unawares, by the breath of God, which we may not recognize. Perhaps it's like suddenly discovering the beauty of Mahler as we move the dial on the radio, or glimpsing a painting and discovering that we are drawn into it. Occasions of joy and wonder prompt us then to look for them, being expectant of them. Not a minute searching, like policemen looking for evidence, but an attitude of heart which makes us welcome them, and not miss them because we are so preoccupied with other matters.

Speaking of 'catching the breath of God' makes it sound as if it is something we do and in a way it is, for the ball will only be caught by the fielder if he is ready, but it is God who reveals or hides himself. He asks for our love and adoration, for us to be open-eyed, open-hearted, wanting to move forward and expectant of his desire to communicate.

God uses the things of this world, His creation after all, as a means of disclosure. At its most heightened and palpable, in the Scriptures and the sacraments, but I believe also in churches themselves. The Scriptures must be read, be broken open, heard in context, prayed, meditated: sacraments need to be approached as meetings with Christ, and should we not approach these churches hoping to find God?

This is the last stanza of Yeats' 'A Prayer for my daughter':

> And may her bridegroom bring her to a house
> Where all's accustomed, ceremonious;
> For arrogance and hatred are the wares
> Peddled in the thoroughfares.
> How but in custom and ceremony
> Are innocence and beauty born?
> Ceremony's a name for the rich horn,
> And custom for the spreading laurel tree.[3]

I find this helpful in understanding our use of churches. In Yeats there is a coming apart to a house, a place set aside for a married couple to live and grow and to become a family in. There's a coming apart by entering a church. The thoroughfare, the chaos, is to be left aside, not to be ignored, but left for the moment. The Church does know what it is doing in building churches, indeed, in using vast resources to build greater churches. They are not an aberration but essential, pointing us to the prodigality of God, His beauty, His joy, what He has wrought for us. Couples need homes: people need churches. I have suggested that the thoroughfare is the place of ordinary commerce, social activity, which we leave aside, but Yeats also regards it as the place of self-centred pride and fear, anger, the small-mindedness, the meanness and closed attitude, but we yearn for the innocence which we have lost and seek to regain through Christ. This, together with goodness, truth, beauty and love, are born in the customs and ceremonies of our earthly home whether marital or ecclesiastical. Doing what Christians do – meeting together, celebrating, praying, assembling sounds and colours and actions into patterns delving deep, not trying to ignore the puzzles and mystery and suffering of life: these are the customs and the ceremonies.

Hatchett describes three levels of ceremonies which accompany the rites of the church – rites, by the way, are words, ceremonies are actions: (1) practical, (2) interpretative, (3) significatory.[4] For example, the entry of ministers, the moving of things required are the practical ceremonies. The manual acts in the Eucharistic prayer, making the sign of the Cross: these are interpretative, and the significatory are things like candles, colour, vestments, incense – things giving and receiving significance (if I understand Hatchett aright). Clearly these latter are adjuncts to the architecture. Piers, carvings, coloured glass are significatory ceremonies even if unmoving. The building is itself ceremonious as well as a shelter from wind, rain, cold and sun.

I find Yeats' words resonate with the image of the Church as the Bride of Christ for Christ brings us home 'where all's accustomed, ceremonious': the Church, building and community, representing and foreshadowing heaven. The rich horn, the cornucopia, overflowing with flowers, fruits, corn, is a symbol of the richness of creation and providence. Surely, that is, there in the greater churches, in music, incense, ceremony and the sheer complexity of the architecture. The spreading laurel is the source and the canopy of honour, of distinction, of glory which Christ gives. Christians perhaps have traditionally thought in images of palms and crowns but Yeats' image gives a greater depth and a freshness.

The prosaic world of today, and of almost every age, scorns custom and ceremony just as it denies the soul. When actually the soul needs to be cherished, and churches are places of that cherishing if we let them speak to us, and we use them aright. If we allow ourselves to be as St Hildgard said: feathers on the breath of God. That we must never forget. God's breath in and around us is the source of all. For He is the one absolute reality. God simply is, and all that is true and beautiful is a reflection and counterpart of Him. In our day this is needed more than ever. For in the desert of so much human living, living which is unreligious, and by being unreligious has shaved away at belief in the inner nature of mankind until it reaches close to vanishing point, man's spirit is atrophied. The Church's mission is not only to keep alive the rumour of God, as someone memorably put it, but to keep alive the rumour of the nature of humankind. This is a truth neglected and diminished by the events of the last century, but beauty is for many the way back.

It seems to me beauty and truth are closely linked. I recall hearing

Michael Ignatieff speaking on Radio 3 (1.2.97) about music teaching us moral truths, by which he said he meant joy, peace, pathos, poignancy. These are emotions, spiritual qualities, which feed our impoverished spirits. We are drawn into music by its truth. For me, listening to a Beethoven Symphony is to be hearing truth, hearing things the way they truly are. And I find this too in the contemporary music of James MacMillan. He has a passionate belief in God and in the moral issues of the world. Pieces like the *Confession of Isobel Gaudie* and his percussion concerto *Veni, veni Emmanuel* have this same quality for me, a quality of truth. And I am reminded of W.H. Auden's poem (p. 238) 'In Praise of Limestone':[5]

> when I try to imagine a faultless love
> or the life to come, what I hear is the murmur
> Of underground streams, what I see is a limestone landscape.

I suppose we may all have different images, but the Western Christian tradition shares the great churches and their liturgy as such an image. I put alongside Beethoven and MacMillan the nave of Lincoln, the crypt at Canterbury, the retroquire of Wells, the shrines of Cuthbert and Alban, and say, for me, these are the way things are: they are true, and therefore speak of God.

The truth expresses itself to us as individuals: for our experiences, our inner self and the external beauty set up vibrations, resonances, and from the ensuing exploration, intuitive rather than analytic, we grow in spirit. The medieval master mason was trying to create an expression of truth, for he was attempting to create a model of the universe and a model of the celestial universe, both of which were patterned by the nature of God – both beauty and truth. More of this when we come to look specifically at the spirituality of Gothic.

In our worship we seek to articulate in words, music, movement, in patterning, something that offers praise and glory to God, but also tries to make sense of the universe, as it is, warts and all. And the buildings are doing the same thing. In *The Bell*, Iris Murdoch describes a visit by Dora to the National Gallery.[6] Dora has escaped from the confines of the lay religious community at Imber Court and gone to London.

> Dora was always moved by the pictures. Today she was moved but in a new way. She marvelled, with a kind of gratitude, that they were still there, and her heart was filled with love for the pictures, their authority, their marvellous generosity, their splendour... She looked at the radiant, sombre, tender, powerful canvas of Gainsborough (his two

daughters) and felt a sudden desire to go down on her knees before it, embracing it, shedding tears. She gave a last look at the painting, still smiling as one might in a temple, favoured, encouraged and loved. Then she turned and began to leave the building. (pp. 190-1)

The sudden desire to go down on our knees before works of beauty is to be resisted, but the 'favoured, encouraged, loved' is to be treasured when we can affirm that it is not the work of art itself which does this but the breath of God catching us, taking our breath away, as we say. At the simplest level we should simply find enjoyment. We need to deepen our capacity for joy, which I suspect we do simply by exercising it. But it is more than that, for these buildings strive to penetrate the heart of things, to tell truth. They give us an inkling (but how glorious even that is) of 'an existence ampler than, and beyond our own'.[7] It stretches us. It gives us dreams to dream. These, however, are not like dreams that vanish as we awake, but a deeper reality than we can otherwise perceive.

In some ways churches are like theatres except there is only a stage and no auditorium, for even if we are eavesdropping on the community at prayer, we are still on stage. I wonder if the English habit of sitting at the back is a way of saying that we would rather be off the stage, and that the clergy, choir, servers are really on the stage? But I repeat, the whole church is stage. It's a kind of permanent set for the permanently running opus Dei with its annual series of variations running from Advent to Advent.

In fact, greater churches are several stages. Let me show you this in St Alban's. We enter by the west doors and look down the nave. This is the first stage: a place for large-scale services, on diocesan and county occasions. Once it was empty, a space for processions and gatherings. But you may notice wall paintings against some of the piers. These were the sites of altars: for when this was a Benedictine abbey, every priest had to say mass every day, and there are numerous places for altars, tiny stages for what was a dialogue between priest and server.

Then comes the rood screen, the rood long gone, but through it we enter the second 'stage': the place of the daily office, now Morning and Evening Prayer but once the full monastic office. The third 'stage' is the open space of the crossing under the central tower and the presbytery beyond. Here is the principle altar for the daily Sung Mass of the community. To north and south of the crossing, transepts with more chapels for low masses, and in the south one, originally the stairs that lead to the dormitory, used by the monks for entering the church for the night office.

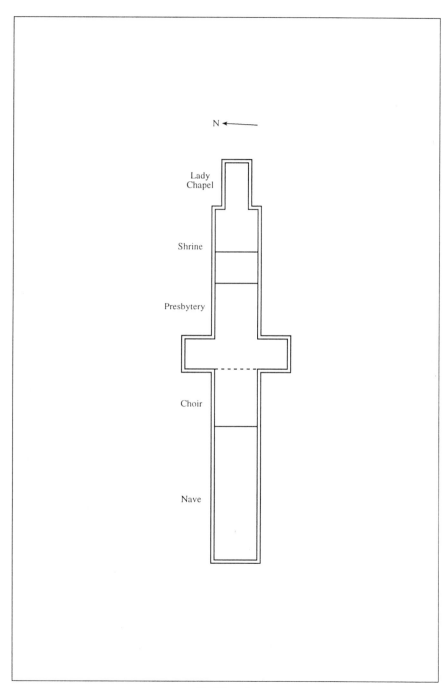

St Alban's.

If we follow around the aisles we come to the fourth 'stage', the Feretory, the place of the shrine of St Alban, a focus of pilgrimage, and a kind of sign of hope, for if Alban can by the grace of God reach the beatific vision of God, then so may we. And he does that in company with the chief of all the saints, Mary the Mother of Jesus, and so the final 'stage' is the Lady Chapel. A place for special liturgies of Our Lady, but again a sign of hope, for the assumed and crowned Virgin is a symbol of the Church and of every Christian. In addition to these stages there are other uses of space: burial, chantry chapels, places of baptism, and beyond the church itself were, and are, the ancillary buildings of the community: the refectory, dormitory, cloister, kitchen, abbot's lodging and so on, now chapter rooms, offices, refectory, toilets, bookshop.

At St Albans this structure of stages is clearly articulated. Portsmouth, the most recently completed Anglican cathedral, although without the screens and on a much smaller scale, also expresses well this sense of movement, of journey, but there are other cathedrals where the punctuation, as it were, has been removed and where the structure of the building as designed has been lost, or at least obscured. Salisbury is such an example and in a different way, St Paul's.

Theatres are neutral spaces as they put on all sorts of productions: *Othello*, *Les Miserables* and *Endgame* might follow one another on three successive nights. But the church is not neutral. At all times it provides a kind of theological backcloth to all the liturgies whether penitential, solemn, joyous, of great formality or easy informality. Always it is there, floor, walls, roof and making a statement both about itself and those who use it.

As we have observed the master mason created an image of heaven and of the universe. The great church is a microcosm, so the floor, walls and roof have a deeper significance: they say something about the place this is. Floors define zones, with varied usage. Sometimes by the use of different materials or different levels. The upward movement at Canterbury, for instance, from nave to shrine. The pavements of marble: medieval ones in Westminster Abbey and around the shrine of St Thomas in Canterbury, Victorian ones in the quire and presbytery of several cathedrals. These mark out important areas, and a few reveal something of local history. The tiles in the retroquire at Winchester mark out the importance of the shrine area too.

Walls are barriers, enclosing and the idea of withdrawal is

important in churches, but walls also say what and who we are. The roof is heaven, and again more important areas may be decorated or have more ornate vaults. I think there is significance in the star vaults in several Lady Chapels. But of course these walls, floors and roofs give us a hint of something far greater, something deeper, an existence that transcends our own and we realize that these buildings go far beyond that which is strictly necessary even for the most elaborate liturgy.

Bishop Richard Holloway in his book *Crossfire* writes about this. In an important coda on worship (and much that I say here and elsewhere is influenced by him), he writes of the philosophic idea of intrinsic goods: things that only have value as themselves, they are not *for* anything. Music is such an intrinsic good. It is its own thing. Prayer and worship are too. He quotes the hymn 'My God, I love thee not/because I hope for heaven thereby' as an expression of this. But he also writes of our impulse to do things, which once had some direct purpose, just for the sake of doing them, for their own sake. As examples he refers to collecting stamps and Trooping the Colour. This ceremony was devised originally so that soldiers would recognize their flag (their colour) in the heat of battle, but our present ceremony, of bands and marching, we do simply for its own sake. It has no purpose other than the delight and joy such things bring.

There are, of course, people who are against these things. The bishop describes them as 'dour and of a puritan disposition, who think that life should be stripped of all these unnecessary flourishes and reduced to strict geometric logic'.

I think we have to reject that view because it fails to see that God Himself is not 'strict geometric logic'. We know God as Creator and the creation is a riot of elaboration, a place of extravagant prodigality. Surely God delights in the sheer exuberance, the overwhelming vastness of the universe even if to Him it is like the nut in Julian's hand which she saw as all that is. From our angle the universe is of extraordinary complexity and the discoveries of science only increase its mystery and its unfathomable nature. The night sky, which has always held a fascination for us, is now revealed as galaxy upon galaxing stretching away into an apparently infinitely expanding universe. I can't get my mind around that, and it reminds me of St Anselm's definition of God as 'that than which nothing greater can be thought'. The American poet, Jeffers Robinson, quoted by Bishop Holloway, says this:

Is it not by his high superfluousness we know
Our God? For to equal a need
Is natural, animal, mineral, but to fling
Rainbows over the rain
And beauty above the moon, and secret rainbows
On the domes of deep sea shells,
And make necessary embrace of breeding
Beautiful also as fire,
Not even the weeds to multiply without blossom
Nor the birds without music.

Something of this 'high superfluousness' is in all art and in the greater churches. The need is simply for a place of shelter for the people of God to meet to worship, but the glass of York Minster, the roof bosses of Norwich, the spire of Salisbury, the ruins of Coventry, that staircase leading to the Chapter House at Wells, these and so much, much more do not meet *needs* but reflect the prodigality of God. They do meet a need in us, the need for living water in our deepest places and the need in us, planted by God, to give adoration and to show love. When I see the hidden glories of nature, or music and painting, my soul smiles, and I recognize God's fingerprint and joy lifts my whole being.

In the greater churches mankind has stretched himself – those high vaults, the huge windows, the entrancing spaces – stretched himself technically and artistically, but most importantly, spiritually. And we too can stand amazed at their ingenuity and skill, but as Robinson indicates our marvelling at the 'rainbows over the rain' points us back to the Creator. I recall a Radio 3 announcer at the end of a concert at which the applause had been especially rapturous saying that he thought some of that applause was for Beethoven. Well, I should hope so. Without the composer where would the performer be? And yes, we may applaud the great master masons but should we not also applaud God?

Mary of Bethany with her pound of very costly anointment, pure nard, is the Gospel exemplar of this adoration. Judas Iscariot asks why it wasn't sold for 300 denarii and the money given to the poor. Jesus told them that they would always have the poor but not always have Him (St John 12.1-8). When I hear people defending apparent extravagance by quoting that story I find myself thinking. We still have the poor, and Jesus implies that this is the time when we do not have Him, so perhaps it is a mistake to mention Mary of Bethany. My mind tells me we should do without and spend our wealth on the poor, but my heart tells me differently. I think motivation of donors and the way we receive is probably the key. As we shall observe in another place the motivation for adding splendour, of raising towers and spires is often mixed to say the least. It was as much about my memorial as God's glory, but if we receive these things as gifts from God to bring us joy and to give us courage to live Christ-like lives then that helps us to meet Judas's objection. The Judases of this world are the ones who miss out. Like the elder son in the Prodigal son parable, they neither appreciate beauty for themselves, nor wish to see others having fun.

If we are able to open ourselves to the beauties and riches of these great churches, not bringing our own agenda to them, but letting their agenda, as it were, come to us, if we embrace them as from God, we find that they make still greater demands on us, open up still deeper capacities. Just as Scripture and sacraments are means of grace so our the churches, but they are not God. These things open up hungers in us which can only be truly satisfied by God Himself.

CHAPTER III

Stone

St Peter writing to Christians new to the faith bids them come to the Lord, our living stone, a stone rejected by humanity but choice and precious in God's eyes. 'Come,' he says, and 'let yourselves be built, as living stones, into a spiritual temple; become a holy priesthood, to offer spiritual sacrifices acceptable to God through Jesus Christ' (1 Peter 2.4-6). Jesus had applied to himself the words of Psalm 118.22: the stone which the builders rejected has become the main corner-stone (Mark 12.10-11). The psalmist probably meant the keystone, the central final part of an arch which holds it all together. Without it the other stones collapse. But St Peter talks about stumbling. You can't stumble against a keystone but you can against a foundation. But whichever, Peter's point is clear: God has chosen Christ as a living stone around whom we as living stones are to be built. The building is a temple in which to offer spiritual sacrifices. It is the Church as a whole, as a community, which offers its worship and we do that in union with Christ. But the fact that the community gathers in a stone building to perform its liturgy adds greatly to the significance of those buildings.

We have seen already that the church building is a sacrament, a sign of the Church based on the Temple of Jerusalem, built by Solomon. The medieval builders were also influenced by the new temple in Ezekiel and John's Revelation. Also that the temple was used as an image of His body by Christ. 'Destroy this temple . . .' (John 2.19-22). The temple of Jerusalem is replaced by the true temple of Christ's Body, and, to use Paul's image, we are the body of Christ. Anatomical image stands alongside architectural, both making the same point. The Christian must be united to Christ.

To the medieval person who lived in a dark hut, at best, without proper windows or chimney, the great stone churches and castles were things of wonder. They are so to us, so to the ordinary men and women of Norman-conquered England, places like Durham or Gloucester must have seemed like something from another world. To be told that this was but a pale shadow of heaven would create a sense of unbelievable joy.

The men who built these churches were undoubtedly people of extraordinary vision. Behind the skills of master masons who were architect, quantity surveyor, engineer, artist, would be a patron, often bishop, abbot or chapter of canons. The patron provided the theological vision but the master masons were the ones who brought that vision to life. They designed the building, chose the materials, solved the technical, engineering problems of stress and strains, and supervised the whole project. They were men of reputation, travelling widely. It was their movements, and the travels of those who worked for them that spread new ideas and new skills.

Master masons were adept in geometry, which undergirds all medieval designs, but they had the practical skills of the craftsman too. Often they would be able to do all the tasks they assigned to others, for they had usually come up through the ranks from being boy apprentices. In addition to stonemasons there were carpenters and joiners, blacksmiths for tools as well as iron work, nails and hinges; plasterers, painters, glaziers, and plumbers, producing lead for roofs as well as pipes. All of these worked under the master mason. Thomas Maude says, 'Wisdom, strength of character, sensitivity and dynamism are all words that could sit easily on the shoulders of the medieval mason'.[1]

There is a parallel here with the Christian community around its head (abbot or bishop) representing Christ. Without unity of purpose, that driving force, these great churches could not have been built.

There is something extraordinarily powerful about stone. It has an imperishability alongside paper, glass, wood or flesh and blood. We know, of course, that the air pollution of the last 200 years has brought stone to crumbling dust but the innards of a stone building survive almost unchanged over nine centuries or more.

The stones are of immense age: 75-175 million years. They were made over millions of years as sediment slowly settled on the seabeds. The fossil bones of shells, the tiny grains of calcium carbonate, rolled over innumerable times in the shallow waters, layers upon layers, compacted; the quartz fragments washed away from the igneous rocks and again settled as sediment, and long, long ago the cooling molten lava, under enormous heat and/or pressure, becoming granite. It took 30 million years to make the stone and probably another 150 million before it was quarried, and carried by water and cart to be built into a great church.

Looking at the stone can add greatly to our enjoyment. A magnifying glass will be a vital tool and a little experience will enable you to tell whether it's limestone, sandstone, Purbeck, flint, or granite.

Christians believe in God as creator. At Morning Prayer each day Psalm 95 is recited. 'Let us raise a shout to triumph to the Rock of our salvation . . . the folds of the hills are his. The dry land fashioned by his hands is his.' Certainly in the nineteenth century the new science of geology caused a crisis of faith in the doctrine of creation, but that is to misunderstand the doctrine of creation. It doesn't say God made everything and then left it, like a craftsman making a watch, or a computer software maker creating a programme, and then leaving it. God is continually involved in the creation, and the timescale is no problem, for the creation stories of Genesis are ways of describing the why and the who, and not the how or when. The stones of our buildings say to us: we were made by God, how great He is, how puny and small you are. We need to learn our place in God's creation. We think too little of God and too much of ourselves. Our colossal pride and conceit are the source of most of our ills, but we are too blind to see it. Of us, a century on, all that will be left is a small pile of dust, or at most a few bones and teeth. God is eternal; we are transitory. The stones tell us if only we will listen that the Lord is indeed mighty. He is 'my stronghold, my fortress, my God, my rock' (Ps. 18.1-2).

The stonemason has tools with evocative names: pitcher, punch, claw, boaster. With these and compass and set square, the stone quarried is made to fit its place in the great design. The voussoirs, for instance, are the stones that form an arch. They each have to be exactly right. Similarly the several stones making up a length of moulding. Each must be chiselled to the same design. The stone is quarried and shaped and the whole structure grows stone by stone, held together by that marvellous substance, lime-mortar. More of that in a moment. And we, as living stones around Christ, have to be shaped and dressed. Life often seems hard. There is much in it that we find painful, hurtful, embarrassing, awkward, but we are being shaped. Listen to these word's:

> Many a blow and biting sculptor
> Fashioned well those stones elect,
> In their places now compacted
> By the heavenly Architect,
> Who therewith hath willed for ever
> That his palace should be decked.[2]

The chisels of circumstance are instruments of God's love, guiding and shaping us. Jesus used the image of the vineyard and the pruning

21

knife, and that says much the same thing. Those moments of loss, of anxiety, of grief, of hard learning, they are opportunities for growth, for being able to be shaped perfectly, so that we may take our place in the world as God plans. The sculptor working from a plain block of stone for a capital at the top of a pillar reveals the design that is within. God the sculptor is chipping away at us to reveal who we truly are. Those builders of centuries ago believed not only that God had created them and this whole world but that he loves it and them. Just as blocks of stone can become a glorious cathedral so we can be stones in the glory of heaven.

Peter began his letter with a hymn of praise to God, 'who in his great mercy has given you a living hope . . . You have not seen him', he writes, 'yet you love him' (v8), and this love is a response to God's love. For it is out of His love that we are born into a living hope. Now let us go back to the lime-mortar.

Thomas Maude tells us about how it is made: it takes six months and then becomes 'a soft, porous and malleable material'. He contrasts that with modern cement used not only by Victorian restorers but even today which is brittle and 'actually strangles the building and speeds up dramatically the decay of all historic buildings'. The thing, which like lime-mortar allows for movement and helps the structure to breath in the living stones, is quite simply love.

Love is the stuff which holds all together as a living structure but all too often there is misused power, fear, an unwillingness to grow together, a rampant individualism and grumbling, which is like the cement, doing untold damage.

The stones of the greater churches can pose us some pertinent questions. If I think of my communities – not just the Church, but where I work, the places in which I take leisure and live, my family – am I allowing myself to be shaped by God to fit together in those communities?

Where in my life are or have been the chisels, the pruning knife and can I see in them the points of revelation, the opportunities for growth and development? Is it brittle cement or malleable lime-mortar that binds me to those around me? Is it creative love or self-centredness that informs my relationships with others?

CHAPTER IV

Glass

If stone seems ageless and unchanging, the coloured glass catches our eyes and imaginations with its brilliance and fragility. The one forms a matrix for the other in a perfectly complementary way. Medieval buildings survive everywhere but glass of that date is pretty rare due to the destruction of reformers and puritans during the Reformation and the Civil War. Glass in itself is also subject to deterioration and decay. The lead in which it is set needs careful restoration but most ancient glass was destroyed by men rather than by time. That which does survive is absolutely glorious, largely deep blues and reds in the early years, and later with gold and yellows. The colours have a thickness about them, but not an opacity. There is also the 'painting on glass' kind of the seventeenth and eighteenth centuries, often imported, and the whole gamut of Victorian stuff. The quality varies enormously both in artistic terms and in condition. Opinions change and there are those who find excellence in windows which were thought vulgar and banal a mere generation ago. The last hundred years has a wide variety of styles: insipid copies, magnificent figurative windows, the abstract, the density and powerful colours returning to some of the riches of the medieval years.

In this chapter I merely try to outline the different purposes that I think windows have and I single out a few examples. The categories are in fact more blurred than this will suggest, but it should help to make things clear overall.

What I ask of you is that you simply look at the glass. Not just in the 'wow' mood nor in the brief glance that says, that's nice or horrid, but in the lingering, staring, dreaming sort of way. If possible find a chair. Contemplating glass is difficult when standing, especially if the window is high up. It's a pity you can't use those walking sticks with seats that country folk use. Allow the glass to speak to you, just as you might listen to music or look at a painting. We only find out what it is saying to us if we pay attention, if we are prepared to absorb it, so the process needs space and time. Really great glass will continue to reveal new insights over the years.

In some cases you will want to identify the figures and the story, but many will be symbolic or even abstract and then it is much more about mood, feelings and emotions.

I think there are three kinds of windows. The first, the simplest designs, are of particular individuals, often biblical characters or saints. Working out who it is is sometimes just a matter of reading a scroll or a plaque in the window. The words may be in Latin and sometimes the script is difficult to decipher, so simply reading may be an overstatement. With some experience you will learn the symbols that are often there: a horned figure is Moses (there is some connection between Moses' face shining and the word for horn in Latin), and a figure with keys will be St Peter. These kind of figures are usually grouped and it can be entertaining trying to work out why those particular people are there.

Biblical stories and the lives and miracles of saints are frequent and form the second kind. These are sometimes arranged typologically. That is to say an Old Testament story is placed alongside one from the New because there is some connection. Moses holding up the serpent in the wilderness and the crucifixion for example. Or manna in the desert and the Last Supper.

The third kind are what, for want of a better word, I call 'theological', and you will know what I mean from that when I describe two such below. And that sort shades off into the abstract. The majority of these windows have elements of figures and symbols but perhaps appear to be abstract at first glance. The nave windows at Coventry might well be seen in this way. So the three kinds are: figures, stories and theological.

Before I give you some illustrations though, a word about the windows themselves. In Romanesque architecture they are relatively small and round-headed. Gothic ones change from simple pointed lancets (often in groups) to ones with complicated tracery. One of the great features of Gothic is the size of the windows: often there is almost no wall. The styles can be roughly categorized as geometric, decorated and perpendicular. The stone patterns themselves are delightful and in some cases symbolic: the heart at the centre of the west window in York, the two 'leaves' of the Bishop's Eye at Lincoln, and the many circular ones. Tracery is better seen from outside where the glass doesn't distract.

The problem with windows is that they are the most easily altered part of a building. It was very easy to change a small window into a larger one and this happened a great deal, so please do not try to date a building simply by its windows.

Many of even the greatest churches will have windows filled with clear glass. They provide floods of natural light, but this is not how the master masons meant their churches to be seen.

Whatever the style of coloured glass and whether we understand the symbolism, the significance and so on, essentially they are stars. Tantalizingly visible, yet painfully unattainable, as Painton Cowens wrote. Edwin Heathcote describes them as 'trailers for paradise'.[1] They capture light itself and make us gasp with joy and delight.

The light passing through the glass makes reflections of the colour within the building. These are so fleeting, so brilliant but so ephemeral as they move imperceptibly from stone to stone, and make flashes of brilliance when they catch the polished, buffed surfaces of marble or brass. And, even some of the worst stuff can make wonderful reflections.

A figurative window, first by W.T. Carter Shapland in the west wall of the nave at Chester. It is easy to 'read' and has vibrant colours and a modern style without being difficult. The window is in perpendicular tracery. The lower half has 8 lights, divided 3, 2, 3 with thicker mullions marking the 2 centre lights. Those mullions divide higher up and go straight to the top and also arch outwards. The heads of the lower-half lights end with five small quatrefoils, then there is a series of oval shapes running across the width of the window and then a great many smaller areas mainly tall and thin, making a total of over 100 areas of coloured glass. The tall lights of the lower half are themselves divided. Elongation of human forms can only be taken to certain lengths, and this is a problem coloured-glass artists often have to deal with. The bottom has scenes of creation and redemption, and then the main areas are six saints with Our Lady and St Joseph in the middle. Thus the Holy Family, for Mary holds Christ, are in those two middle lights marked off from the rest. To the left are: Werburga, Oswald and Aidan: the foundress of Chester Abbey, and the king and the missionary he brought from Iona to preach the Faith in the north. To the right are Chad, Wilfred and Etheldreda, saints associated with the Midlands, Yorkshire and Eastern England. All are local and of the same heroic period of the English Church's history. The scenes below relate to the saints above and we get one of those typological pairings as Mary is linked with Adam and Eve: Mary frequently described as the second Eve, and her obedience countering the disobedience of the first. The upper half has a great many symbolic elements. Some I guess are obvious like the three red circles against a blaze of gold for the Holy Trinity. The sun and moon are much used symbols of time, but the Greek letters for Jesus Christ and Victor are not obvious. Indeed a great many Christian symbols require explanation. They come to be symbols, as it were, only to those who know the story. Whereas there are symbols which are universal and speak directly to almost any human person: water, bread, kingship, for example.

For the story windows I choose the great east window at York. It is about the size of a tennis court and was made by John Thornton of Coventry in the years 1405-8. It has a total of 305 openings, and remains the largest area of ancient glass in England. The technical skills employed were formidable and the overall artistic achievement makes this a masterpiece of a very high order. From afar it shimmers with blue light, like a vivid mosaic but close to, and I think binoculars are a must to appreciate it, the scenes are designed with a remarkable freshness and the whole has a tremendous vitality. The tracery panels at the top include the nine orders of angels, Patriarchs, the heroes of Israel, Prophets and Christian Saints. Then there are the rows of square panels. The first three tell the story from Creation to the Apocalypse. A story told regularly in the liturgy but also more familiarly to the folk of York in the Mystery Plays, some of which are still performed in the city each summer. Below that, and in far greater detail, the rest of the window tells the story of the Book of Revelation: eighty-one panels in all. The bottom row has kings, saints, Archbishops of York, and in the centre the donor of the window, Bishop Skirlaw of Durham (1388-1406). I had wondered if he was well pleased with his gift, but he died before it was finished.

As you will have seen, already we are moving into the theological, for telling the story in this way is a theological statement.

The rose window in the north-east transept at Canterbury dates from the late twelfth century and makes a more direct theological statement. It shows the Old Dispensation: the central square (that in itself is interesting because the square in medieval geometry is a sign of God) has Moses and the Synagogue: Law and worship. There are then 4 triangular panels which have the 4 cardinal virtues (again 4 as in the sides of the square); and beyond that the 4 semi-circles have the Prophets, and all is set in a circle, which represents the cosmos, and the whole window is a rose. That too is a symbol of Our Lady, and of Paradise. Perhaps we tend to think of the Old Testament as superseded by the New. Rather we should see it as the first act of a two-act drama: the Old Testament leads to the New. In it we see the pale reflections of New Testament events. This becomes clearer as we explore the typology stuff, and see how the OT is used in the Lectionary.

Finally from a medieval window to one completed in 1997 and after a battle in the courts: the John Hayward window in the West wall of Sherborne Abbey.

The patron saint of the Abbey is the Blessed Virgin Mary and the Incarnation is, appropriately, the subject of the window. Now that could be depicted by a scene of the nativity but in fact Hayward's window tells the story of the purposes of the Incarnation. Heavier mullions divide the window into three sections vertically, and this is used to allow different scales in the inner and outer sections. At the bottom we see the branches of a tree with fruit. The serpent is twined round the branches and has a fruit in its mouth. Then the branches become a background, grid-like, for Mary as the 'Christ-bearer'. The Genesis story of the Fall and humanity's loss of innocence is shown. 'At the advent of the Child the Redeemer, the Tree throws up new shoots on either side, and blossoms. There is a roof above, a house of clay.'[2] In the next stage the tree becomes the Cross and there is a canopy of the empty shroud. Against the Cross is the dove of the Holy Spirit which we can read as descending from the blaze of the Father's glory above onto the Virgin and Child, but also as a participator, as it were, in the mystery of Redemption: the doctrine of coinherence. (That, very summarily put, says that each member of the Trinity is involved in all its activities.) The Cross breaks into new growth and becomes the Tree of Life. Above is the sunburst of God the Father as the source of both Creation and Redemption. 'God was in Christ reconciling the world,' as St Paul says. So here, caught in a single moment, as it were, is the story of creation, man's disobedience, Mary's obedience, and Christ's act of redemption in the cross and resurrection and all of this in the context of the Holy Trinity.

To the left are the Magi showing the nature of Christ as king, priest and victim, and with more originality, the shepherds, to the right, as the Green Man, Good Shepherd and Light of the world. Hayward quotes the saying of Jesus: 'Raise the stone and thou shalt find me, Cleave the wood and I am there.' We are reminded here that the qualities we see in Christ are also to be in us, his followers: bringing illumination, tender, compassionate, loving and, especially as the Church, revealing Christ's presence everywhere. Below there are the two Johns: poet and prophet, with quotations from the Gospels: The Word was made flesh . . . and Behold the Lamb of God . . .

John Hayward also has the scales of justice in the bottom right corner – a reference to the legal battle that had to be fought to allow his window to replace an earlier one, which despite its poor quality many people, and not least the Victorian Society, wished to preserve. There are many other small details in the window. The one I especially like is the depiction of the Hale Bopp Comet, which appeared whilst the window was being made. Sherborne has here a wonderful window, with superb glass, but also with sensitivity and imagination, a source of teaching for future generations to tease out.

St John in his first letter writes this:

> God is light, and in him is no darkness at all. If we claim to be sharing in his life while we go on living in darkness, our words and our lives are a lie. But if we live in the light as he himself is in the light, then we share a common life, and the blood of Jesus his Son cleanses us from all sin. (John 1.5-7)

Actually it is not as clear cut as all that. Much more about shades of grey than the simple dark or light. We need to be honest about the shadows in us – the dark side of our personalities, which we keep hidden away under some kind of lock and key. The light of God wants us to uncover the shadows, discover more about them, and to allow that light to penetrate. It is a fact that shadows only come with light: and perhaps we can only know our dark spots, the things that bring shame and hurt, when brought to the light of God's love. So there are questions about dark and light in our lives, but the glass of the churches is brought to life by the light passing through. Only with light from beyond do they shine in their glory. And this is true of us too. On our own, we are a bit dull and lifeless, but transformed by the Holy Spirit we can become adazzle. Christians' lives do not draw attention to themselves but are activities and silences, words and thoughts and prayers through which God is revealed. If glass is a trailer for paradise, then our lives can be trailers for God, if we allow His light to shine through us. Words of Jesus sum this up: Like the lamp, you must shed light among your fellows, so that, when they see the good you do, they may give praise to your Father in heaven (Matthew 5.16). You will notice there that the others are not drawn to you, but seeing good, give praise to God. We are not to get in the way: we are to let God shine through us just as light shines through the glass.

The statue-covered west screen at Wells Cathedral.

The extraordinarily elegant nave at Lincoln, with its use of Purbeck stone to contrast with the local limestone.

This Christus is by Peter Eugene Ball, and hangs above the nave in Southwell Minster.

This Corona celebrates the resurrection in the central tower at Hereford Cathedral.

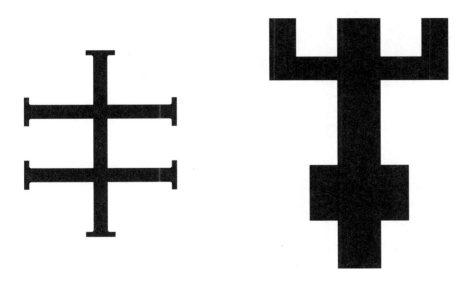

Liverpool and Guildford use these cross-shapes based on the ground plan of the two cathedrals as logos.

At the centre of this cross is a smaller cross made from medieval nails that fell from the roof of Coventry Cathedral as it burned after attack by the Luftwaffe.

CHAPTER V

Facades and Porches – the Way In

Greater churches nearly always have several points of entry. Ordinary visitors and regular worshippers rarely use the most important, the grand entrance – the West Doors. These are reserved for very significant occasions; perhaps the enthronement of the bishop, or a visit by the Queen. In a few places you don't enter the church itself. Chester funnels you through a heritage display area and you find the church only via the cloisters. Salisbury too, and Oxford have other entry points. However, even if the main entrance isn't open and you can't go through it it is a place to be explored. The facade and entrance is saying something important about the place you are entering. Just as the towers and spires signal a place of importance from the distance as they soar above the roofs of the city, so here there will be clues to the sort of place we are entering.

God's story is often told there in statues and carvings. A number of places have what can only be described as an image screen. There will be prophets, the men of faith who foretold the coming of the Christ. There will be Apostles, who were called by Christ and then empowered by the gift of the Holy Spirit to lead the Church's ministry. Their successors are the bishops so they have a special significance on cathedral churches. Martyrs and saints also take their places recalling the universal nature of the Catholic Church and its mark of holiness. Angels too are common, and at the heart of all this is Christ Himself. There are three typical guises for Him: as a Child with His Mother, in judgement or in blessing and welcome. 'Christ will come again,' we affirm in the Eucharist, and that coming reminds us of the challenge of the Gospel and that our response may bring us to nothing or to salvation. This is the place where the Gospel is proclaimed, the Christ is preached, the sacraments are celebrated and where Christ may be experienced.

Kings, benefactors, founders, other historical figures are often portrayed and, of course, patron saints. Relatively few greater churches are dedicated to saints other than Mary, but for example, the triple dedication (Andrew, Peter and Paul) is shown in carvings on the west facade at Peterborough.

Some of these west facades are very plain and with almost no sculpture. Others, and especially Lichfield, Salisbury, Exeter and Wells have great screens of figures, once brilliantly coloured. Evidence for this has been found in restoration work at all these places. All these facades, and the clear glass screen at Coventry with its figures engraved, are worth our attention, and in many different ways they 'set the scene' for our encounters within.

Porches are places of crossing boundaries but also places of shelter and protection. They are both a way in and a way out. Crossing the threshold is not always easy. The cathedral narthex in Sheffield has four sides: three are ways out, only one is a way in. That speaks to me of this difficulty for many folk.

The threshold is a key place and we need threshold people. Jim Cotter reminds us that boundary people are sometimes eccentric and often unpredictable. 'Valuable because they have come to be at home in the wilderness and are able to guide others through a bewildering time of transition'.[1] They are kinds of midwives, helping not only for things to come to birth, but also helping us to cope with the dislocation that comes with transitions into new areas.

Often doors in huge facades are tiny. At Wells one feels them as a necessary interruption, but the medieval thought was that doors represented Christ who had said He was the door of the sheepfold (John 10.7) and therefore both the apostles and the bishops, who are the shepherds of the flock and so seek to fulfil that same role.

The great porches are known as Galilees. This is the area of northern Palestine where Jesus spent the principle part of His life and, according to the Synoptic Gospels, most of His ministry. It's His home base, the place of teaching and miracles, the place of calling disciples (for many of whom it was also home).

After the Resurrection the angel at the empty tomb told the women that Christ had been raised and was 'going on before you into Galilee; there you will see him' (Matthew 28.7 and Mark 16.7), and so in Matthew's Gospel the disciples travel north and meet Jesus at the mountain 'where Jesus had told them to expect him', (Matthew 28.16), and there He gives them the mission to make disciples everywhere. John, chapter 21 is also set in Galilee. A group of seven disciples have gone fishing and caught nothing. There in the early morning light they see a figure on the beach with a small fire. He bids them to try letting down their nets again and this time there are so many fish the nets begin to break. He calls them to breakfast, and, of course, this is Jesus. After breakfast Jesus asks Peter twice whether he loves Him, and then, whether he is even His friend and Peter is given his special task of leadership (John 21.15f).

This going to Galilee then is to meet Christ and to be commissioned for ministry. The Galilee porches are part of the route for the procession of the Sunday Mass and the antiphon uses words from Matthew 28. The Galilee is the place leading into worship and meeting Christ. The disciples had to travel north to meet Christ. We go to church to hear the Gospel, to receive the Blessed Sacrament and then to go back to our homes and the rest of our living, for that is where we are to minister. Porches, remember, are places of entering but also of leaving. We shall only discover the full significance of these facades and porches when we enter and get involved.

CHAPTER VI

The Nave – the People's Church

The laity are all the people of God, which includes the clergy (bishops, priests and deacons) but when we use the word laity we are normally excluding the clergy. Cathedral priories, abbeys and even prebendal churches are not designed primarily for the laity. They had their own churches, served by their own priests and often nearby. In Lincoln there was St Margaret's within the Close, St Mary Magdalene, St Paul and St Michael and St Peter just over the close wall, all within less than 200m from the cathedral. St Thomas' is the splendid parish church five minutes or so walking distance from the cathedral in Salisbury and St Michael-le-Belfrey almost touches the Minster in York.

In the medieval parish church the liturgy was relatively simple and the contrast between those and the greater churches became greater after the Reformation. The music was the principle difference. In the parishes almost nothing apart from some metrical versions of the psalms were sung and organs were very rare until the nineteenth century, although many had the bands of instrumentalists. Thomas Hardy recorded them in one of his novels. In the cathedrals there were polyphonic anthems and service settings and the organ. Not until the nineteenth century did larger parish churches, and some not so large, attempt to ape the greater churches, with organs and robed choirs in the chancel.

The Cathedral Close at Norwich was itself a parish – St Mary in the Marsh – which had existed before the diocesan centre was moved from Elmham, via Thetford, to the city in 1095. The church was destroyed in 1570 and the Chapel of St Luke in the cathedral, plus the nearby aisle on occasions, became their parish church. The font was brought with the people to make a point of the continuity. Parishes need fonts: cathedrals rarely so. The parish of St Cross in Ely had a building north of the nave, a lean-to affair, and from 1566, that having been demolished, they moved into the Lady Chapel, and renamed it Holy Trinity. It was only returned to the Dean and Chapter in the 1930s. Similarly in Chester the south transept was a parish church from the 1530s till 1881. In some places the adjacent church survives. St Nicolas in Rochester and St Margaret at Westminster, for example, and the latter, parish and abbey, are staffed and administered jointly.

A number of greater churches survived the Reformation only by becoming parish churches. Those which have subsequently been raised to cathedral status have retained their parish identity too. The Dean of St Albans is also Rector, for example. However, with the exception of the Cistercian churches the naves of greater churches had always been open to lay people. The Cistercians were the exception for two reasons: first, the nave was used by the lay brothers of the community, and second, the churches were so remote there was no local laity to attend.

However, over the years cathedrals have come to have congregations: those who choose to worship there, some because a member of their family is part of the foundation; some because they prefer that style of worship; others after rows in their parishes; some because they prefer the anonymity of the cathedral. On the whole until very recently there were no parochial-type activities for worshippers to be dragooned into, and that was an attraction for some. The report 'Heritage and Renewal' suggests that such people 'not be regarded by others as refugees from surrounding churches but as bridges between the cathedral and the rest of the diocese'.[1]

Only at Southwell and Ripon (95 per cent and 76 per cent respectively) do a sizeable proportion of regular worshippers come from the local community. For a great many cathedrals, especially those in the commercial and shopping centres of large cities, few people will be resident in the local area. Michael Perham reckons that at Norwich, in addition to the members of the foundation, the regular worshippers number between 200 and 300.[2] In summer in major cathedrals (those on the tourist route), there may well be 500-plus and at the principle Eucharist the casual visitors will outnumber the regulars.

The point about cathedrals and abbeys (real ones, I mean, with monks) as well as collegiate churches like Westminster, is that the Liturgy does not need a congregation. The Liturgy will be performed day by day in its elaborate way simply for God and the sanctification of those who take part, and as an act of intercession, but it no more requires 'outsiders' than does a parish Eucharist.

There are, though, great services at which lay people come in great numbers: diocesan occasions, and county, civic and community organization sponsored services: Christingles, Advent and Epiphany processions, judges services, harvest festivals. In Coventry a service for those hurt and killed in road accidents is held. People who have been to these sorts of services find them inspiring and come away spiritually enriched. Precentors and cathedral musicians give a great deal of time and expertise to make these sort of events as telling as they often are.

The nave, although part of the consecrated church, was often a place used by laity for other purposes than worship. Trevelyan described parish naves in the middle ages, when they were, of course, largely empty of furnishings, as village halls. J.G. Davies says, 'it is difficult to think of any secular activity that had no connection with naves.'[3] That is as true of cathedral naves. After all they were the largest roofed space in any town or city until recent times.

Guilds met there. Fairs were held in Salisbury and Ely. So profane were the uses of the nave of Old St Paul's that the Lord Mayor issued a proclamation 'For Preventing of Profanation and Abuse' offered in St Paul's. That in the sixteenth century. It's twelve-bay nave was a market and a thoroughfare. It became known as Paul's Walk – a popular resort for Londoners about town to swap gossip, to see and be seen. Johnson's play of 1599, *Every Man Out of His Humour*, sets Acts III in St Paul's nave. The characters include two gallants, a dog, and a cat in a bag. People also used the nave to stick up advertisements, a kind of free advertising journal. As late as 1841 Sidney Smith said, 'the whole thing resembles more a promenade in a ball-room than a congregation in the house of God'. This suggests that the celebration of worship in the quire didn't cause the people in the nave to behave any differently. And what was true of London, was to a lesser extent true of York and Durham.

Less profane were ecclesiastical courts usually held in a chapel. The south-west chapel in Lincoln, now a shop, was a consistory court, and Chester's has been preserved under the south-west tower. Many issues were brought before those courts: inquests, seekers of sanctuary, payments of debt, pluralities, tithes. In Norwich rents were paid on the tomb of Chancellor Spenser wearing away the stone. The Bauchon Chapel there, originally called Our Lady of Pity, gets its name from one William Bauchon. He was corn storekeeper to the priory and paid for the chapel (£14 17s 4d) in 1327-9. The vault was added later, about 1470, and paid for by William Seckington, advocate in the consistory court. His arms and face appear, as do scenes from Chaucer's *Man of Lawes' Tale*, but also the Assumption and Coronation of the Virgin.

The benefactor is the reason for the legal images rather than its later use as the consistory court.

Today university degree ceremonies are common and concerts, plays, exhibitions are frequent. In the spring of 1998 I came by chance across a medieval banquet being set up, children attending a prize-giving, other children preparing for a service to commemorate an anniversary of their school, several concert rehearsals and a major flower festival being dismantled, and a display of GCSE and A level artwork.

In the smaller cathedrals the nave is used for regular Sunday worship and the larger ones need to use the nave in summer because of the numbers who come, but I do plead with dean and chapters to empty their naves of chairs as often as possible. There are problems of where to store chairs, and there are so many events which need them. The naves of York, of Salisbury, of Exeter, of Canterbury and many more gain immeasurably from being open and free of furniture. The naves of Liverpool and, on a much smaller scale, of Portsmouth are very much separate areas. In Liverpool the floor, known locally as the swimming pool, is several feet below the level of the aisles and flights of steps lead down to the nave. The bridge across the building forms a wonderful punctuation mark.

These naves can be places of dialogue – the Christian faith with anything else prepared to engage in dialogue on church territory. Christ sends us to proclaim the Gospel, everywhere, to everyone but that means listening as well, trying to build bridges of understanding. All of good will and perhaps even those who are not, should be welcome. And not just to deal with 'religious' issues. If the Church is not concerned with every aspect of human life it is failing the Incarnation. Naves can be a catechumenate state, an extension of the porch, places of discovery, or awakening, of decision, but they are never neutral spaces. That is why the west facade or any main entrance needs to signal clearly that this is a Christian Church, a place of liturgy, of prayer, and alongside the signs asking for money (the average request is for £2.50 per adult – tickets tend to be more) there should be ones with a warning: coming in here may change your life. Almost everywhere there are people who welcome you and hand you a leaflet. In some places the welcomers stand very close to the donation chests, and at a discreet distance in others. It is right that we are welcomed, although I feel this place is my home anyway, but we are guests and perhaps should remember that when our hosts are not as prepared to receive us as we would like. St Benedict said of the monastery 'guests are never wanting' (RB 53,16) and in that chapter of the Rule he reminds the community that guests are to be welcomed like Christ (53.1) and especially is this true of 'poor people and pilgrims' (53.15).

CHAPTER VII

Crucifixion and Resurrection

The Gospel story reaches its climax with the Passion of Christ. That part of the story so dominates the whole that someone once described the first 13 chapters of St Mark's Gospel as a great up-beat to the Passion narrative in chapters 14 and 15.

The story is told with a remarkable austerity: plenty of details, incorporating, one feels, the evidence of eye-witnesses, but narrated without comment and with a sharp, direct language devoid of emotion.

Jesus celebrates the Passover meal with his disciples in an upper room. We, mindful of what is to follow, see this 'last supper' through the events of Good Friday, but to those men it was the joyous annual celebration of their ancestors' escape from slavery in Egypt. Moses led those ill-tempered, recalcitrant, unbelieving slaves across the Red Sea into the wilderness of Sinai. Every Jew sitting at the family table eating the unleavened bread, the roast lamb and bitter herbs, sharing the glass of wine at the end, was, thereby, crossing the Red Sea, being delivered from slavery, from darkness, from evil, into the freedom, light and goodness of God. They remembered these long ago events and thus were themselves delivered.

Jesus sounded a new music there at that Passover table. The prayer of thanksgiving, the *berakah*, was transformed, renewed when he said, 'This is my body' of the bread, and when the cup of wine was offered to all, 'This is my blood'. The Passover was being rewritten. What did the disciples make of all that? They were utterly mystified by Jesus' references to betrayal even when Judas left the room prematurely. St John's 'and it was night' strikes cold in our hearts.

Then singing the traditional psalms, they leave the room. From the flickering candles they go to the darkness of an olive grove lit by the rays of the Passover moon, soon to be filled with noise and the glare of torches; Jesus is bound and taken away. There was no-one to watch for the disciples all ran away, including the young man in St Mark's account who, grabbed by the soldiers, escaped their hold by leaving the cloth he was wrapped in and running away naked.

Mockery, trial, torture, scourging, the way of sorrow, the nails of crucifixion followed and Jesus hung naked in the bright sunlight the next day, bearing not just the physical agony, but far more painful, the sin of the world. No wonder the world became dark (Mark 15.33) and finally He cried out, 'It is finished, it is accomplished,' and died.

The wounded, bloody, broken body, lacerated by the metal tips of the scourge, bruised by the soldiers' brutality, drained of colour, was taken carefully down. The thorns of the mock crown gently removed, even now that they could hurt no more, and Jesus still warm, but oh so dead, wrapped in linen and laid nearby in a tomb hewn from the rock. The great stone was rolled into place and sealed, guarded by soldiers. The women among Jesus' company watched from a distance.

The Cross has been turned from being a symbol of criminal execution in the rough justice of the Roman Empire into a sign of glory. Most of our greater churches are cross-shaped. The feet of Jesus at the western doors, His arms across the transepts, His head at the high altar. Very few are actually as simple as that, for some have a second cross form in the eastern arm itself and other additions obscure the cross-shape. Liverpool and Guildford use their differing cross shapes as symbols of the cathedral.

Once all the great churches had naves dominated by the Rood: Jesus crucified, with His mother and St John below. The figures were high above the rood screen with its altar below forming the sanctuary of the nave. Not surprisingly these nave altars were often in honour of the Holy Cross. All were destroyed at the Reformation. Only one rood screen survives, at St Alban's, and there probably only because it is stone and not the usual wood.

Now only a handful have roods: Westminster Cathedral, Peterborough, a bland effete example at Wells, and another small one in Chester. Southwell has a carving by Peter Ball. It is high up, remote, awe-inspiring but I suspect so high up that it is not seen by many. It has a Byzantine quality, austere, hieratic.

'Those great spaces were not meant to be filled with chandeliers, but with the life and death and life again,' writes Pamela Tudor-Craig.[1] If only . . .

Llandaff commissioned a Majestas from Sir Jacob Epstein. It commands the whole nave but mysteriously has no wounds. I think of it as a Christ of the Transfiguration but it has a tremendous spiritual quality as with almost all of Epstein's work.

The Sutherland tapestry in Coventry is certainly the King of Glory, but clearly too the Cross has not been ignored. The lower section forms a reredos for the Lady chapel, oddly for such a place, but shows Sutherland's genius in representing the Crucifixion in grim realism.

Stations of the Cross are even rarer than crucifixes. Westminster Cathedral has the most marvellous set by Eric Gill, and Sean Rice, a Liverpool artist, who died in 1997, created a new set for the Metropolitan Cathedral there. The figures are set within silver framing, against a black background. They are dramatic, filled with carefully observed detail, and, just being looked at, highly effective. But stations are liturgical. They are meant to be *used* as a focus of worship. In the first, where Pontius Pilate washes his hands, a slave kneels and Jesus is very still and majestic. One is reminded of the dialogue about kingship between these two men in St John's Gospel. In the fourth, Mary touches the crown of thorns, and in the fifth Simon is really helping support the weight of the Cross. In the seventh there is dynamic movement as if the fall is down through the air. The same kind of dynamic is in the thirteenth. Jesus' body is being lowered on ropes and the soldiers are quite acrobatic, one sitting on the top of the Cross. And the last has the tomb in the background. Joseph and Nicodemus hold the emaciated dead body with such tenderness. I found these stations among the most moving I have ever seen.

Blyth Priory has a recent set hung in the north aisle. They are not, however, set out individually, but grouped together. According to a guide in the church when I visited, they are not used liturgically, but such use would be difficult from the way they are arranged. They are semi-abstract and repay contemplation. They were painted by Druie Bowett who lives in the village.

Southwell has a Pietà in the south transept, and also an Ecce Homo in one of the chapels. The finest though is in the ruins at Coventry. Epstein's is made of Subiaco marble which is a white colour and stands in contrast to the reddy brown stone of the old cathedral. It is weathering too so has some areas that are greenish. The stone is 'blocked' and the hands bound with ropes hang down. From the side the figure appears squat and there is an African quality to it, both in the posture and in the facial features. The hands reveal Christ's acceptance, His willing obedience. This is not a man being taken to death against His will. There is nothing of struggle, just the deep pain of suffering endured. That is enormously encouraging to all who suffer, for our suffering endured as Christ's was, and offered with His to the Father, becomes transfigured. The statue faces north towards the new cathedral. That and the nearby tower and spire pointing heavenward give added meaning to Epstein's work: crucifixion leads to resurrection. Good emerges and evil is redeemed.

The lack of images of the Crucifixion or the dead Christ is because of the Resurrection. But that is not the whole answer. There is more which I see in my ministry as a parish priest. There are folk who go with Christ through Holy Week. People who come to the Stations, who stand at the foot of the Cross on Good Friday, but far more who seem somehow to be able to skirt around the Cross, but still come to celebrate the Resurrection. This is something I cannot understand.

If the nave is a place of dialogue with the world it must still be a place that speaks of Christ and the fact of His Crucifixion on a particular Friday, in a particular city, under Pontius Pilate, as the creed puts it, fixing it firmly in world history. That fact has to be confronted by all who come into dialogue with the Christian faith.

On the wall near the flight of steps up into the porch at Coventry is the other Epstein sculpture there – St Michael and the Devil. Obviously it is about the triumph of good over evil, but I always think of the passage in Revelation which describes this: 'And there was war in heaven . . . ' (12.7f) as a kind of parallel with the death and Resurrection of Jesus. This sculpture is another way of expressing the Easter mystery. Coventry is in a sense a vivid symbol of this whole thing, for to turn from the ruins and to go down the steps and face the great glass screen and through it to see the Christ in Majesty is to travel from Calvary to the Easter garden, from death to resurrection.

How we do theology about this I find almost impossible to express, but I know it is at the core of my Christian experience. I can't fathom it but I know that I'm forgiven. That is an experience given us, if we are fortunate, in childhood when our parents forgive us and their body language if nothing else tells us. And that, long before we learn to say 'sorry'. I now find this same experience of God. Like the father in Jesus' parable, he runs to meet me, throws his arms around me and orders the preparations for the party, smothering my rehearsed, but hesitant confessions. I know there's something much deeper in repentance but I also know deep within me that God forgives and it has some direct, profound, even if inexplicable link, with the death and resurrection of Jesus. And it is not only forgiveness. The things wrong with me are more than just my deliberate wrong-doings. Sin in the Old Testament often means missing the mark and I know the 'mark' is to be whole, complete, fulfilled. Redemption is that process by which God works in me to heal the wounds, to allow the fulfilment of the possibilities life has, and in the end, for me to become

Christlike. That is a process to which I shall return to when we come to shrines and chantries, but for the moment let me say that it is vital for our redemption that we engage positively, constructively with the Cross. Like two cogged wheels – a small one being driven by another, often on a different plane (and in this case a finite with an infinite), my life needs to cog with Christ's.

Greater churches that somehow hide the Crucifixion are offering less than the Gospel however well Christ is preached there or the Liturgy proclaiming His death is celebrated. And please, not remote, golden crosses, but ones in which we see the pain of the world reflected.

Those who suffer deeply, the pain of rejection, of betrayal, the wounds of abuse or neglect, the cold indifference of people around them, the watching of pain in a dying child or parents, these people need the crucifix. I think of Julian of Norwich's revelations, coming at a time of suffering, as the priest held the crucifix before her when she saw the blood dripping from Christ's head like rain off eaves, His draining of colour, and His being dead. Through all that, mysterious and dark as it is, come the words of hope: And all shall be well, and all manner of thing shall be well. And only because of the Cross of Christ.

I think these words were originally St Augustine's but they echo repeatedly down the ages. 'We are the Easter people and Alleluia is our song.' If you like, we live in the Easter garden.

The Christian year changes dramatically at Easter. For Benedict's monks it was the point at which the daily pattern changed and he gives a chapter (15) on the singing of Alleluias. 'From the holy feast of Easter until Pentecost alleluia is always to be said with both psalms and responsories.' He also gives the alleluia treatment to every Sunday of the year except in Lent, and all because of the Resurrection.

The strongest evidence for the Resurrection is the Church itself. The transformation of Peter and his companions from frightened, timid folk into people of heroic faith isn't easily otherwise explained.

The Gospels tell the Passion story, as we have observed, with restraint, with meticulous detail and without emotion, but the Resurrection accounts are so different. You can't chart Jesus' appearances in parallel columns. You can't reduce the narratives to simple history, what actually happened. For this is a unique event: literally, a one-off. Father Aidan CR says it is like a mighty firework. 'You light the touch paper and run for cover behind a wall.' Getting caught up in resurrection is certainly like that but it is God's life exploding into our world and resurrection is all around us.

Towers and spires shooting skywards, huge windows of brilliant glass throwing light inwards, exuberance of decoration and carving, even now when the blues, reds, greens and golds have gone: all these shout Alleluia. It is this joy that is much lacking in human lives. No wonder millions of people are drawn to the great churches for there they find joy. We need to learn again to enjoy things, to keep our eyes open and expect to be enriched by the experiences life gives us. Dom Philip Jebb says, 'For myself I really believe God loves me, and is constantly thinking up new ways to bring me joy, as is the way of all true lovers'.[2] He writes of joy as the object of life and points out that if you are always looking for dangers and pitfalls you'll never see the view and 'if you try to skate without falling over you will never know what skating really means'. And isn't that the spirit of our great churches? The freedom, and joy and occasionally the bumping of elbows and spines on the ice. For from time to time towers collapsed, or a vault didn't quite work (think of the one over St Hugh's Quire in Lincoln), but most of them are the apparently effortless joy of the skater.

In a sense it is the whole church which speaks to us of the Easter mystery, but there are some specific things as well. Lincoln has a beautifully carved Easter tomb to the north side of the Presbytery, used in the dramatic Easter Liturgy which eventually grew into the mystery plays. Glass with images of the Risen Christ is frequently to be found. Ely has a sculpture by David Wynne of Christ with Mary Magdalene in the garden, and in a completely different way, in a different medium, Sutherland's painting *Noli me tangeri* in Chichester addresses the same subject. Typically though Sutherland captures not just the immediate moment of recognition in the garden, but by its angles and setting, by the staircase and the image of the Father, points us both back into Jesus' earthly ministry and towards the Ascension which is referred to in the Gospel account of this incident. 'I am ascending to my Father and your Father.'

Hereford Cathedral decided to create something to mark the end of John Eastaugh's episcopate. It was commissioned by the Friends and they asked the bishop for his thoughts. He wrote that he wanted it 'to reflect the power of the Holy Spirit and the hope and joy of the Resurrection and Ascension'. As that ancient hymn which St Paul quotes in his letter to the Philippians suggests the exaltation of Christ is theologically one event (resurrection and ascension) and the outpouring of the Holy Spirit is the fruit of it (Philippians 2.6-11). That kind of understanding is also seen in John 20, where the Risen Christ appears and breathes on the disciples the Holy Spirit. Hope and joy are two elements key in Christian lives lived between the exaltation of Christ and His coming in glory. Simon Beer accepted the commission and produced the corona to hang above the new altar in the crossing. Hereford is a cathedral without a screen and the corona makes an important point of punctuation. There is a German tradition of coronas, known as *Die Raidleuter*, wheel of light. Amongst the most famous is that in the Cathedral at Aachen and there are contemporary ones in Blackburn and Liverpool Metropolitan. Usually they are places to provide actual light and this is true in Hereford. Candles are lit at all main services. The corona is gold and silver and like the altar a pointed oval in shape. Romanesque detail is part of the altar design and these are to be found in the corona too, thus echoing the rhythms of the cathedral. The oval shape is also found in the Gothic windows of the transept. Interestingly the Precentor of Hereford, Paul Iles, writing in a pamphlet about it says candles make 'the Corona shine with bright flames and their reflections'. But goes on to remark that unlit its character changes according to the light available in the building. 'It can be as much a crown of thorns as a crown of sovereignty and glory.'[3] The death and resurrection of Jesus are the stuff of our worship so now let us pass through the screen, into the quire, and come to the heart of what greater churches are about.

A pulpitum stands at the west end of the Quire. Often the organ is placed above. This one is at Southwell.

The Blessed Sacrament Chapel in the Metropolitan Cathedral in Liverpool.
The designs are by Ceri Richards.

The shrine of St Alban has recently been decorated with this embroidered cover. It is based on what we know of medieval shrines.

The tomb of the Venerable Bede in the Galilee Chapel at the west end of Durham Cathedral.

53

This is the plinth on which once was enshrined the head of St Hugh,
at Lincoln.

These steps lead up from the Quire aisle towards the Shrine of St Thomas at Canterbury.

CHAPTER VIII

The Quire

The bell has ceased to toll. The time is almost 5.30. The organ is playing quietly and a small congregation waits in the stalls of the quire. Then rises to its feet as the choir of boys and men in scarlet cassocks and long-sleeved white surplices walks in, filing naturally into their places. The altar is reverenced. All turn and bow to the Dean, the organ falls silent and into that silence a minor canon sings: O Lord, open thou our lips. The master of the music's fingers move and the choir respond: And our mouth shall proclaim your praise.

Thus day by day begins Evensong in English cathedrals. Psalms are sung, two readings of scripture heard, canticles are performed, creed recited, prayers said. An unchanging rhythm daily which has continued in this form since the Prayer Book of 1549 except for a brief break during the Commonwealth. But the tradition goes back much further than that; 1549 saw a dramatic change of gear but the daily praise of God goes back to the foundation of these greater churches, some as long ago as the sixth century. This is what St Benedict called the opus Dei – the work of God, and this is the essential purpose of these churches. Whatever kind of community, Benedictine, Augustinian canons, Cistercian monks, secular canons, the office was celebrated daily at regular intervals both day and night.

These services grew out of the Jewish morning and evening prayers which the early Church had retained, and this became the 'cathedral' tradition. The services were sung daily by the bishop and his household, publically in the main church of a city. But when the monastic movement got well under way and religious communities were established they developed a whole series of services to mark the hours of the day. The first, Matins and Lauds, was in the night: then at the various hours, Prime, Terce, Sext and None (taking their names from the 1st, 3rd, 6th and 9th hours of the Roman day) and then as dusk came Vespers, and immediately before bed Compline to round off the day. This corresponded to the psalmist's 'Seven times a day do I praise you' and 'at midnight I rise to praise you'. The cathedral office was simply taken over by the monastic one and it wasn't until the revisions of Archbishop Cranmer in the sixteenth century that the

56

cathedrals, which were now all staffed by secular canons, reduced the services to two, which together with the Eucharist form the daily pattern everywhere. It is good that others join the cathedral community but the cathedral is doing its central and vital work when just the members of the foundation are there saying their prayers. Evensong will be sung just as well, just as ornately, whether there is a congregation or not. For God is always there and it is this particular community offering its worship.

The part of the greater church where the opus Dei is celebrated is the quire. To reach it in many places you pass through a screen. All of the churches originally had two screens: the western one was nearly always wooden and above it was the great Crucifix, and in front of it a nave altar. Then beyond it a solid stone screen, known as the pulpitum. The difference between the two is that rood screens have two doors, on either side of the altar, and the pulpitum has one central one. St Alban's is a rare survival of a rood screen, but pulpitums survive in a great many churches. Others have more open screens of wood or metal, which replaced older pulpitums which had been removed, and a few places, notably Hereford and Salisbury have removed all screens making the quire open to the nave. The pulpitum is a symbol of monastic enclosure: the shutting out of the world. It has practical points too, like reducing noise and draughts. Jesus told us that when we pray we should go into our private room and shut the door (Matthew 6.6). This is what we are doing by going into the quire.

Some quires are quite intimate spaces; I think of Chichester, but others are huge, like Canterbury or Lincoln. It rather depended on the size of the community. The rear stalls, and those with their backs to the pulpitum, which are called returned stalls, are for the Dean and Chapter and for prebendaries or honorary canons. The Dean and Precentor usually have stalls at the west end of the quire, the Chancellor and the Treasurer at the east: sitting as it were at the four corners, literally so at Chichester and Lichfield where the stalls are all on the east-west axis. Above the stalls in the secular foundations are inscribed the titles of the prebends. That word is related to provisions, and was used of the income, in rents or goods, from an estate. The income was for the canon to live on – his stipend, or prebend – and so there were as many prebends as there were canons, the number usually being fixed by the bishop. The titles are therefore places. In Lincoln you will see names of places far away from the modern diocese, for once it stretched from the Humber to the Thames. In monastic churches, or those of regular canons, it was the community which had income, not the individual monk or canon and so there were no prebendaries, and the stalls were allotted by seniority. At Ely, the bishop was abbot and so he sat in the principle stall, the first on the south side, and still does, despite the abolition of the monastery long ago. Those cathedrals which were refounded in the sixteenth century had a reduced number of canons from the number of monks or regular canons of medieval days, and all the cathedrals have had reductions in staffing down the centuries. What we now have in addition to the Dean and Chapter (usually a total of 4) are honorary canons and prebends. The bishop appoints clergy to be honorary canons. They are usually senior staff in the diocese and it is a kind of long-service honour. Each honorary canon or prebend (there is no longer any income to go with it) has a stall assigned to him which he may use when he comes to the cathedral. A few cathedrals have lay canons and a number provide stalls for heads of schools, architects, heads of nearby theological colleges, and so on. The greater churches which are simply parish churches may well have the stalls but they have no canons for they are no longer that kind of community. It is the residential staff of the cathedral; together with the minor canons (clergy to sing services and sometimes to be chaplains to the cathedral congregation) who together with the choir are responsible for the daily worship.

Choirs are varied in origin: in some of the ancient cathedrals there have been singing boys since their foundation. In the monastic churches they sang with the monks, until the stage where the music became too complicated for the average monk to sing. The prebends and regular canons faced the same problem and so then vicars choral were invented. Vicars because they are deputies of the monks or canons, and choral because they sang – as they still do. Some houses and certainly the Cistercians, never had choirs as such and retained the simpler plainsong. In recent years a number of cathedrals have formed girls choirs as well, and many of the men who sing are choral scholars associated with universities nearby.

If you stand in any of these quires and look around, you will see the stalls. They are places of human scale set aside for a particular person. The canopies are practical, to keep out some of the draughts. Heating in these churches has only been there for about a century. But here is a place, with desk, seat, place for books, for a person to say his prayers in, and from which to join in the corporate worship. In parishes people often have their favourite seat, and get criticized for it. I can see that no-one should object if someone else is in their seat, but I can't see why it should be wrong for people to have his or her place. It has to do with a sense of belonging. In the greater church quire the stall is a place within a family and helps with our need for roots and stability.

I remember an elderly member of the regular congregation in Chichester saying as he saw someone was sitting in his usual place, 'How shall I sing the Lord's song in a strange place?' But he said it with humour and happily found himself another place.

The seats of many stalls are hinged, like seats in cinemas and theatres, but not so that people can pass along the rows more easily. These are hinged so that when up, the person occupying the seat can rest his posterior on the ledge provided, so that although he appears to stand, he is actually being supported. These are known as misericords, a word having to do with taking pity. The offices were long and this was a help to monks and prebends singing the offices. Beneath the seats, and to be seen when they are up, are wonderful carvings. Some of these are among the finest medieval wood carvings in England. They include, as you would expect, religious scenes, but these are invariably in a minority. The whole of life is there: animals like monkeys, fox, owl, lions and mythical ones, like gryphons and dragons. Scenes from famous stories like Tristan and Iseult, wrestlers, a sow playing bagpipes, a quarrelling couple, a stag and hounds, a goat playing a lute – these are just some examples and show the imagination of the carvers. There is often a grim sense of humour as well as a keen sense of life. The medieval world saw itself whole: the idea of sacred and profane division didn't occur to them, and these carvings, often derived from manuscript illuminations, show their delight in the whole of life. We need too to find that holistic attitude to living: our lives so often divided into compartments and lacking a sense of unity. If you want to explore misericords you will need permission, for often the stalls are roped off, and you'll need a good torch and a nimble body to be able to get into the right positions. The best sets are probably Lincoln, Hereford, Chester and Manchester, although those in Hexham are easy to see. The pulpitums are usually wonderfully carved and decorated with statues of kings, archbishops, saints, so do look at those too.

The stalls face each other across the quire and the choir sings as it were in two halves. This derives from the poetic nature of the Hebrew psalms. Every verse is in two halves, usually of equal length, and the two halves either say the same thing in different words, or are in opposition to each other.

So the palms are recited by the two sides of the choir, using alternate verses, which is called antiphonally. I suspect originally it was actually by half verses. William Byrd described this as being like a tennis game, hitting the ball back and forth across the net.

The music is one of the glorious parts of English heritage and its practitioners are highly skilled musicians. The amount of music sung is vast and the repertoire has extended enormously in the past thirty years or so. Most choirs sing music from every century since the sixteenth as well as the plainsong which goes back to the early centuries of the Church. There is a great deal of pressure on cathedral music, economic as well as social. The costs are rising rapidly, and the commitment required to sing almost daily for a great part of the year, creates difficulties. But there is no doubt that it is sung better, and with a wider repertoire, than ever before. As Gilbert Thurlow has written, 'it would be villainy for any technologically obsessed generation to destroy this tradition'. Or even worse, for it to perish because we are not prepared to pay for it.

When he retired after twenty-seven years as organist at Canterbury Allan Wicks was asked about abiding memories. 'Oh, little things,' he said. 'The sound of the psalms being chanted on one of those dog-days in midwinter, when there's not many people about and the sound in the cathedral is particularly thrilling.'[1] That it seems to me is what it is all about and we Christians who are not part of greater church foundations can learn from it.

We need that regularity of prayer, day by day. We need to create some kind of pattern that fits our lives, and that will almost certainly need to be changed from time to time. And added to the pattern, a place or places. I'd like to suggest finding a space in a church, but as they are nearly all locked that's not much use. But just as the monk or canon has his stall, so we need our place. Find somewhere in your home which can be a praying place. It doesn't have to be large: perhaps a cushion with an icon or crucifix on the wall, and a candle to burn.

Another thing I think we can profitably learn from the office in cathedrals is the centrality of the psalms. In the Rule of St Benedict he is prepared to cut down on readings, but never on the psalms. He says of his monks who recited the 150 psalms in a week: 'We do, indeed, read that our holy fathers in their zeal carried out in a single day what I trust we lukewarm people may accomplish in a whole week' (RB 18.25). Well, he might think us stone cold, even frozen, but we are not monks and we have the rest of our vocation to live, whether teacher, cleaner, mother, carer, city analyst or whatever and prayer for us is just a part of the work we do for God, our opus Dei. The psalms are, however, after the Gospels, the most fecund part of the Scriptures. They are a rich vein to mine and however slowly we work through them they will bring us rich rewards. Benedict says 'we believe that God's presence is everywhere . . . especially ought we to believe this, without the slightest doubt, when we are celebrating the divine office. Let us consider, then, how we ought to behave in the presence of God and his angels , and stand and sing the psalms in such a way that our mind and voice may be in harmony' (RB 19.1-2, 6-7). He also says in his next chapter that prayer should 'be short and pure' (RB 20.4). The place and the time of our praying can create stability for us, but the second Benedictine vow is conversion of life, and that is about change and growth, and that is what our praying should be about. The roots go deep to draw up the nourishment of the soil, but the nourishment is there so that we may grow tall in the sun and produce flowers and fruit.

At the heart of Lauds and Vespers are two canticles: those we know by their Latin opening words, Benedictus and Magnificat. They are both from St Luke's Gospel: the words of Zechariah at the birth of John the Baptist and those of Mary when she visits her cousin Elizabeth (Luke 1.67-79 and 1.46-55). They come the other way round in the Gospel. In the modern Liturgy the Benedictus comes in Morning Prayer and the Magnificat is one of two canticles in Evensong. They are sources of deep meditation, and their daily use over the centuries points to this richness. The Magnificat is about the Incarnation, the coming of Christ and the overturning of the ways of the world in his life. The Benedictus, is about the promises of God being fulfilled.

The daily prayers of the greater church community mark and sanctify the time. They run in cycles, daily, weekly, yearly. They reflect the rhythms of life. Perhaps we can let the place of this prayer, the quire, influence our own praying so that we too may make holy all our time.

CHAPTER IX

A House for an Altar

I suppose the title of this chapter is the definition of a church but certainly one of the distinguishing features of greater churches is their numerous altars. In addition to the main ones in nave and presbytery and lady chapel there were lots of small chapels off transepts, ambulatories and sometimes against pillars in the nave, or in the nave aisles, all with their own altars. In many of these churches recent years have seen these altars replaced and chapels refurnished. This large number of altars says something about the importance of the Mass in the medieval period, and indeed the Eucharist is *the* form of our common worship. The rite is extraordinarily flexible, from celebrations with one or two people, entirely said and with chunks of silence, in a small chapel in the early morning at one, to those exuberant occasions with music (choirs, trumpets as well as organ), a vast congregation, many ministers in rich vestments, candles, incense and a deep sense of the catholicity of the Church at the other. Such occasions might be a provincial festival in York Minster or an ordination, the small ones happening every day.

The intention with which the Mass is offered runs the whole gamut of human life and experience: from the grief of a requiem, to a thanksgiving for the Resurrection, from prayer for a new-born baby who is ill, to a celebration of fifty years' priestly ministry.

The Eucharist has been the centre of liturgical renewal. That is where most of our attention has been focussed and we still have much way to go in our renewal of non-Eucharistic worship. Books like *Celebrating Common Prayer*, produced by the Franciscans, and the Taize liturgies point the way but the Church of England is officially far from that.

The greater churches celebrate the Eucharist day by day: a double focus of Christ's presence in the Scriptures and in bread and wine; and a rite which contains all the elements of prayer: adoration, intercession, confession and thanksgiving.

For our medieval ancestors, awareness of what was going on in a rite conducted in a language most didn't understand was 'by cues provided by the choreography in the chancel with the climax at the elevation of the Host'. R.N. Swanson cites examples of parallel prayers.[1] For example, after the Sanctus:

> Lord, you should he honoured; with all my heart I worship you, as I well ought, for more good than I can know which I have received from you since the time I was conceived . . . Then the time of sacring is near. People usually ring a little bell; then you shall pay reverence to Jesus Christ's own presence which may loose all baleful bonds. Kneeling, hold up both your hands and so behold the elevation.

Everyone knew that 'of all things in the world, the mass is the worthiest thing of most goodness', and being present was enough.

It was a piety based on meditation within a rich environment in carvings, glass, wall paintings and statuary. Interiors were filled with colour in what might seem to us now a kind of gaudy, fairground style. A few places attempt to revive this, for example the Lady Chapel in Bristol Cathedral, and a good many Victorian parish churches were similarly decorated.

Medieval religion was centred in Christ. The stories of His life and passion were very well known. The mystery plays, although using apocryphal material and having a great deal of humour and irony, were still deeply embued with the Gospel. That is in marked contrast to modern-day retellings in musicals and films which tend to distort and simply get things wrong. This is a problem for the Church. We have to find new ways of enabling people to hear the story, as the Gospels tell it. Dorothy L. Sayers' *A Man Born To Be King* did this extremely well for an earlier generation. But to return to the Middle Ages: the crucifix was everywhere. All worshippers stood beneath the great roods and people were drawn into the reality, the cruelty and pain of Christ in centuries where pain was largely unrelieved. Julian of Norwich's *Revelations* are drawn out from the crucifix being held before her by the parish priest when she seemed to be dying. She writes of seeing Jesus' blood drop like rain off the eaves, and the pattern reminding her of the scales on a herring seen in Norwich market.

The liturgical year, then as now, took worshippers through the whole of Christian doctrine, as again the Mystery Plays did, from Creation to the Last Judgement.

The basic prayers known by heart were the Lord's Prayer, the Apostles' Creed and the Hail Mary. We fail to understand these medieval churches, shorn now of their colour and vitality, if we do not perceive how the saints and especially Our Lady, were closely woven into ordinary people's everyday lives. There were Marian prayer books and the lives of the saints were well known from books, sermons, coloured glass. The intercessions of the saints were for them a real power: something which perhaps we are beginning to appreciate again.

There was an understanding of *koinonia* – the Church united in heaven and earth – in which the intercessions of the Liturgy are matched by the prayers of the saints in heaven, but everyone knew that it was God who acted. Praying 'to' is a misuse of the word, and it is better if we reserve that only for communication with God.

Recent liturgical revision has brought into use the commemoration of saints and with men and women of recent years. I try when introducing the Mass on these occasions not just to tell the story but to tease out something of the spirituality of the person. Cathedrals which house shrines or are dedicated in honour of people could make much more of this and some are already doing so. It can be done in liturgy and in books and sermons, but also in works of art. The tapestry designed by Ursula Benker-Schirmer in Chichester is an example. She writes of discovering the life of St Richard and the Dean also suggested some central Christian symbols: chalice, fish, fig tree and candle. 'Gradually, the symbols and biblical verses began to cohere and a pattern of meaning established itself as a kind of personal leit-motif.'[2] 'It is my earnest hope,' she says, 'that the tapestry will move the observer towards reflection and meditation.' It has a playful gladness and joy, making an affirmative world view.

In the end the saint's life is a pattern of Christian living, of the Gospel realized, so the fundamentals are often the same. The lives of individual saints are like light refracted through a prism. No doubt each age finds echoes and resonances of itself, its concerns and issues, and that is certainly true of the Calendar 2000.

Devotion to the Blessed Sacrament greatly increased in the thirteenth century. The feast of Corpus Christi was established to provide an occasion of thanksgiving for the Mass which was inappropriate on Maundy Thursday. This was a great holiday-feast with processions, flowers, the Host, placed in an ornate monstrance, carried aloft, incense, lights and much singing. An occasion in which lay folk would take an important part.

As I have observed the death and resurrection of Jesus were central. They remain so, for the Cross is the means of redemption. Much medieval religion had elements of superstition and abuses in relics and indulgences abounded towards the end of the period, but alongside the forgers and money-grubbers there were the saints, the ordinary folk of deep piety. We can't go back even if we wanted to, and I'm certain we shouldn't even want to. We live today and look to the future. Jesus Christ is, as Hebrews says, the same yesterday, today and for ever. The reality of Christian faith is the same but must be clothed in the ways of our own generation, but we would be missing out a great deal if we ignore what the things of the past which have come to us can contribute to our worship, our spirituality.

There is a need for great sensitivity in how we use these buildings. We always need to ask, why were they built as they were and how does that help us to understand more deeply what we are about? Churches must not become museums, they must live and change if they are to be sources of spiritual growth for people today and in the future.

CHAPTER X

Extensions for Saints

A great many churches rebuilt the eastern arm, often not long after the original build. This was not only to lengthen the presbytery for more complicated ceremonies but to house the shrine of a local saint. Sometimes this was done in the hope of getting a saint, and space for the hoped-for pilgrims.

At Ely the presbytery was rebuilt in 1234-52 to house the shrine of its Saxon founder, St Etheldreda. The shrine is now marked by an enscribed slab and four candles, and is before the high altar. In the original design the shrine was east of the high altar, separated by a reredos screen, and there was another screen beyond the feretory (the word from the Latin for bier which was given to the shrine area) separating that from the five eastern chapels. That screen was on the site of the present reredos, so the shrine site is unaltered. All the other feretories are still east of the high altar. Notable examples are at St Alban's, Winchester, Chichester and Lincoln.

At Lincoln, the chevet east end, built by St Hugh, was demolished to make way for a large, square-ended building. The pairs of chapels off the eastern transept survived, but the central five went. St Hugh actually had two shrines: one in the usual position, east of the High Altar, and the other by a pier on the north side. This was the shrine of St Hugh's Head. The modern additions were added in 1986 to mark the 800th anniversary of Hugh becoming Bishop of Lincoln.

St Swithun's shrine at Winchester extends much further east. This 'nave and aisles' type space made for many more burial places as well as for the pilgrims who came to the shrine. Canterbury's extension, built above the extended crypt, is the Trinity Chapel. This retains the ambulatory shape of a chevet and has one central, almost circular chapel at its eastern-most extremity. Canterbury then has a direct route around the shrine area, which helped it cope with the great many pilgrims who came. For this was the pilgrim church par excellence in England.

The news of the murder of the Archbishop, said to have been carried out at the command of the King, in the cathedral, swept like fire across the whole of Europe. Henry II and Thomas Becket had a

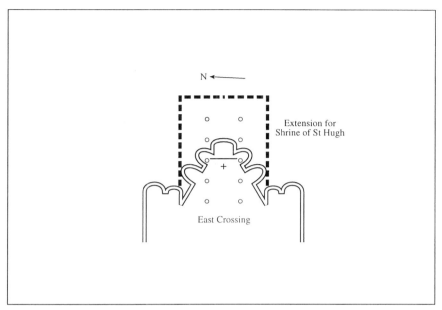

Lincoln.

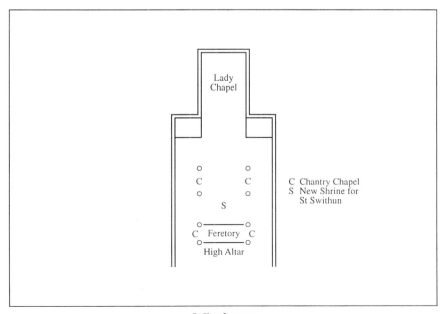

Winchester.

unique relationship. It had begun as youthful pursuit of sports, especially riding and hunting, developed through a period of collaboration when Thomas became Chancellor, and then the period of division and argument when Thomas, on being made Archbishop, ceased abruptly to be the King's man and became obstinately, proudly, God's man. Henry's power was thwarted at almost every step by the claims of the Church and that these claims were expressed so fervently, so unbendingly by his erstwhile friend made the King's anger all the deeper. I doubt that the words 'who will rid me of this turbulent priest?' were said with the serious intent of provoking murder, but four knights left Normandy, where Henry was keeping Christmas, crossed the Channel and made inland to Canterbury. The Archbishop was confronted at first in his palace, but as darkness fell on that December afternoon in 1170, the knights, fully armed, returned as the community prepared for Vespers. The Archbishop came through the cloister and into the north transept, and there the knights found him. He had insisted that the cathedral doors remained open. Perhaps he was courting martyrdom, but there, near the door that leads into the crypt, Thomas was killed. Later Henry came barefoot to Thomas' tomb in the centre of the crypt and was flogged by one of the monks.

Almost immediately after his burial miracles began to occur and Thomas was canonized in 1172. Two years later the cathedral suffered a major fire. I guess the cathedral would have been rebuilt anyway, for the crypt was not a suitable place for a major shrine, but the fire provided the ideal opportunity. Between 1175 and 1184 the whole of the eastern arm was rebuilt and extended. We have an eye-witness account which provides remarkable details. The story is told well, with illustrations in Tim Tatton-Brown.[1] Canterbury already had several shrines: Dunstan, Alphege and Anselm among them, but their importance paled beside Thomas. Despite his martyrdom and the glory both it and the new eastern extension had brought, the years between 1184 and 1215 were hard for the Benedictine priory. King John and two archbishops, Baldwin and Hubert Walter, were in constant disputes and the whole community spent the years 1207-13 in exile in France.

Canterbury is a flat site but from the nave the pilgrim moves ever upward to the shrine. From the transepts flights of steps rise into the quire aisles, which are very wide. Then, as the quire itself narrows, at the point where the Norman quire ended, there are more steps. In the presbytery these steps lead first to the high altar and then a further set to the level of the Trinity Chapel where the Chair of Augustine now stands. In the north aisle you can see how the steps bury an earlier blind arcade, for the original ambulatory continued at the same level. The new building retained the old foundations and outer walls because of the crypt beneath. Just off these steps a door to the south leads into a small chamber, called the Wax Chamber. It is now the Vesturer's Office and is directly below the Chair, but it has windows into the eastern crypt and was probably a watching chamber for the first shrine. The pilgrims pass up those steps, smoothed with use, to the Trinity Chapel.

This is a remarkable area of extraordinary richness. There are double columns of Purbeck and another pink marble which so far has not been identified. There is a pavement of Italian marble-inlay and in the centre was the shrine, renowned for its extravagance. Tim Tatton-Brown has worked out that the three steps of the podium were laid flat in the pavement when the shrine was destroyed in 1538. Now the site is marked by an inscription. It remains one of the holy places of Christendom. Architecturally this is the climax of the cathedral, but there is as it were a coda, for beyond the ambulatory, is the Corona, now a Chapel of the Saints and Martyrs of our own day. It was created as the place to enshrine the piece of Thomas' skull sliced off by one of the knights. The present dedication reminds us that more people have died for their faith in the twentieth century than in any other.

Richard in Chichester, Swithun at Winchester, Cuthbert and Bede in Durham are among the other shrines to which pilgrims travel. So we are led to ask, who are the saints and why do people go on pilgrimage?

The saints are people who now experience the joy of heaven. The Roman Catholic Church canonizes those whom she believes to be in heaven. The Anglican Communion has no such process and in its calendar lists men and women in two categories: those who have lesser feasts and those who may simply be commemorated, probably by some reference in the intercessions. A fifty-year rule applies except for martyrs. That is, you may not be added to the calendar until you have been dead for fifty years, and the Church is quick to point out that these are not 'saints' in the Roman sense. Canonization certainly is a response to what people believe about someone, and that is true of some of the Anglican names. It is an issue that the Church ought to give some attention, for are we really saying that there have been no saints in our Church since the split from Rome?

To our medieval ancestors the saints were the focus of a great deal of their living. The saints were the most powerful intercessors, led by the Blessed Virgin, and the chief purpose of pilgrimage to a shrine was to seek the saints' help.

The Creed affirms that 'we believe in the Communion of Saints'. This phrase is a filling out of our belief in the Church. The Church is in essence a community, *koinonia*. A community created by God and given life by the Holy Spirit. It is the Holy Spirit which makes us all holy – *hagioi*, in the New Testament, the saints. In the New Testament the saints are simply the Christian community, those people called by God to be with Jesus and to be sent out into the world in mission. You and I are saints. But hang on, I hear you say, we are not saints like Julian of Norwich, Francis or Thomas Becket. And you are right. We use this same word to describe those whose lives and deaths have shown what being a saint ought to mean. They are not only intercessors for us and with us, but also examples to us. Their heroic lives give us hope and courage. They are a pattern to inspire us. When we read and contemplate their stories we find a new energy to continue our own living. This energy is, of course, God's grace flowing to us. We see God in the saints. They are witnesses to His way by their living, as much as by their deaths. The word martyr is the Greek word for witness. Those martyrs now celebrated in the Corona at Canterbury were witnesses in a world of violence, turbulence and passion, to the truth of God and by remembering them, by dedicating a chapel in their honour, we are allowing their witness to continue. Jesus said, Unless a grain of wheat falls on the ground and dies, it remains a single grain: but, if it dies, it yields a rich harvest (John 12.24). Remembering and honouring saints is a part of the crop.

We desire to be like them, that our faith may grow stronger and our love run deeper, and by their prayers and example, grace flows to us. St Therese of Lisieux said: 'I want to spend my heaven in doing good on earth' (The Final Conversations, 102).

The chief of all the saints is St Mary, the Mother of Christ. Some greater churches are dedicated in her honour, and those which are not have Lady Chapels. 'Our Lady' was a title drawn from the language of romance and courtly love, taken up by the Cistercians who dedicated all their churches to Mary, and whose white robes were adopted as a sign of her purity.

Lady Chapels are nearly always the easternmost part of the church. Examples which are not, like Ely and Canterbury, I'll mention later. In the majority the pattern is the same: either high altar, shrine, Lady Chapel, or in some cases simply high altar and then Lady Chapel. There is significance in this position.

Firstly, because it is eastward. Turning eastward has become something forgotten in the last thirty years, but orientation is deeply significant. Those in church who were facing north or south, would turn to face the altar at certain points in the services, and the vast majority of churches are built so that when facing the altar one is facing east. The east is the place of the rising sun, and thus symbolic of the coming of Christ. Psalm 19.5 reads: 'In the deep has he set a pavilion for the sun, it comes forth as a bridegroom, it rejoices like a champion.' The psalm goes on to link this to the message of God's glory: 'They have no words, nor voice, but their message of the firmament goes everywhere.' Bridegroom and champion are much used as images of Christ, and is He not the champion of the poor, the downtrodden, the oppressed? Every morning at Lauds, and in the Anglican liturgies at Morning Prayer, the Benedictus is recited. It has phrases about the dawn from on high breaking upon us and those in darkness and death being shone upon. And this too is about the coming of Christ who enlightens everyone (John 1.9). The liturgical focus is always the altar and that is usually east of the congregation, except in the rare churches where the altar is central. (Only Liverpool Metropolitan among the greater churches has a central altar.) The altar too is the place of Christ's coming, in bread and wine. The season of Advent presents us with this same double edge: remembering the coming of Christ in time, but also looking for His coming in glory. There is a lovely carol with this refrain:

> People, look East, and sing today;
> Love the guest is on the way.[2]

And in subsequent verses Love is identified as rose, bird, star and Lord. So looking east is with an attitude of expectancy. The Nicene Creed's last clause says: We look for the resurrection of the dead and the life of the world to come. In Latin this is 'expecto resurrectionem mortuorum'. The looking is active.

In Portsmouth Cathedral beyond the principle altar is the St Thomas' Chapel where, above the altar and beneath a rich canopy, the Blessed Sacrament is reserved. David Stancliffe, the then Provost of Portsmouth reminds us that God calls us not just to be members of His Church but that 'He calls us to move beyond that, to recognize that He is Lord, not only of the Church, but of the whole world, and that His kingdom extends beyond anything that we can conceive or comprehend.'[3] So beyond the high altar there is the hanging pyx 'containing the Sacrament as a focus of Christ's presence among us, yet lifted up from us'. The Church does not stop with Easter: the ascended Christ leads us on and points us heavenward. Filled with the Holy Spirit we have a mission in the world to help bring in the kingdom.

I think the Portsmouth hanging pyx is a splendid focus of this eastward thrust – heaven and kingdom on earth. Worship always leads us, kicks us, out into God's world 'to live and work to His praise and glory' , but in doing that to further the kingdom.

Do not the lives of the saints point in the same direction? Their holiness, their Christlikeness, their beatitude draws us beyond Easter to Ascension and heaven. In them we see redemption fulfilled. They are holy and whole, and their lives are now linked with the worship of the angels and archangels whose lives simply burn with continuous praise and adoration of God, the Holy Trinity.

The saints by their intercession for us, with Christ's who according to Hebrews ever lives to intercede for us, they 'fix the whole Church more firmly in holiness as they proffer the merit which they acquired on earth through the one mediator between God and man, Christ Jesus, so by their fraternal concern is our weakness greatly helped'.[4] St Dominic told his brothers that he would be more helpful to them after his death than when alive. 'I shall help you then more effectively,' he said.

Their lives on earth though point us back to our living, in family, in school, places of work, in our social and political lives: in the hard places where we confront our pain, our weakness, our shattered illusions, and in the places of delight and joy, and growth in love. The kingdom is to be built in this world but can only be built with our eyes heavenward. Christ is the one whom we follow, who journeys with us, but we journey together, in community, with the people of God here and now, but surrounded by a great cloud of witnesses (Hebrews 12.1). If we will let them the saints are very much engaged in our journey with us.

The assumption and coronation of the Virgin seem to some extravagant doctrines but in truth they are the pattern which we are called to share. Mary, like all humanity, is redeemed by the death and resurrection of Christ and so passes from this life into heaven. Her life of humble obedience, of unmurmuring, joyful acceptance of both glory and pain is the example to us of Christian living. We see all the virtues in Mary and faith, hope and love lived out in what on the surface seemed a very ordinary life, but when contemplated is a life of extraordinary grace. We are all to be crowned: remember the twenty-four elders in Revelation 4, and the royal priesthood of 1 Peter (2.9) To lay their crowns before the throne is a symbol of worship but they have crowns because God has called them into the royal priesthood, the chosen people, whose task it is to proclaim Christ's triumphs: being called out of darkness into marvellous light. That is the Gospel.

The saints and especially Mary find their rightful symbolic place beyond the high altar: the Lady Chapel is itself a shrine to give us hope and encouragement. We give thanks to God for Alban, Cuthbert, Werburga, Chad and Mary – and with their prayers and God's grace from the altar and looking to the future we return to our places (T.S. Eliot).[5] A shrine is a place of hallowed memory – a place of relics, the body of a saint, but remains hallowed even when the body has been destroyed. The bodies of Edward Confessor and Cuthbert are rare survivors, but to stand at the place where the tomb stood, knowing of its destruction, makes an altogether stronger message. We have to be silent and let the mystery of the saint speak to us.

Every Lady Chapel is a shrine to Our Lady. Nearly all have glass, or reredos, or statues of her. These are important as witnesses to her holiness and influence and these are further reflected in the architecture. One frequent feature of Lady Chapels is that they are lower in height than the main building. Designed for the medieval liturgy of Our Lady they are usually much longer than other chapels as places not for a priest and tiny congregation but for a communal liturgy. This lesser architectural style seems to me a symbol of Mary's lowliness and obedience. It also makes these chapels more homely, reminding us as Walsingham does, that Mary was wife and mother in a real home in Nazareth. In some they have a distinct separation from the main building, but in others there is a movement of spatial freedom.

This is especially so at Wells where the retroquire was designed for a shrine, but William of March, the hoped-for saint, was never canonized. The architecture is very interesting. At first sight the Lady Chapel seems to be a single bay with a three-sided apse, but look up at the vault. There one discovers that it is an elongated octagon. The star shape is frequent in lierne vaults but recalls the hymn '*Ave maris stella*' 'Hail, star of the sea', and the vault is actually a star now painted with a star. Christ enthroned on the central boss points to the fact that Mary's place entirely depends on Him. The retroquire is an even more elongated hexagon, but with its vaulting and placing of pillars makes for a series of extraordinary vistas. The vault which can't be described in words according to Pevsner[6] is like a piece of complicated polyphonic music. Look for the lions. They bite off three ribs that proved unnecessary.

Two Lady Chapels are not eastern extensions, Durham and Ely, and Canterbury has two chapels, off the north transept and in the centre of the western crypt. At Durham a chapel was built across the great western doors of the cathedral and overhangs the cliff above the River Wear. It is said that attempts to build the chapel at the east were thwarted by Cuthbert's mysogony but I think that an odd story. And maybe when the Chapel of the Nine Altars was built beyond Cuthbert's feretory the central chapel was dedicated to Mary.

The western one is known as the Galilee Chapel as if it were a porch. But it may well have served the same function as there are doors into it from both nave aisles. It has had a Lady altar since the late twelfth century. It was a consistory court from the fourteenth century. It still houses the tomb of the Venerable Bede.

At Ely a huge chapel was constructed to the north of the quire. It is five bays long, and I wonder if this is a reference to the then very popular devotion of the five joys of Mary. A handful of other lady chapels are also five bayed. The impression today is of a building flooded with clear light, but that is not how it was conceived. The windows were filled with coloured glass and the carvings above the niched stalls were painted in bright colours. M.R. James studied the iconography of the damaged carvings and they are drawn mainly from the apocryphal Gospel known as Pseudo-Matthaei. This chapel speaks to me of the ambivalent attitude to the Virgin in the Anglican Church: the refusal by many to give her any honour for fear of placing her above Christ, but at the time, losing out on so much. We can't change the past, but we can learn from it and grow out of it. We may regret the destruction by puritans of glass and sculpture, but we can rejoice in the marvellous light that fills this chapel on even dull days, and in the tracery of the windows which is seen so well against the clear glass. And let's not fret about the corporate sponsors whose names are recorded in the windows. Just think of heraldic emblems, which in a much brighter key, are the same kind of thing.

Canterbury's two chapels are called Our Lady Martyrdom, because it is near the site of Thomas' death, and Our Lady Undercroft.

I would like to believe that the dedications of the crypt chapels in Canterbury make some kind of sense but it remains a mystery to me. The Lady Chapel is almost exactly under the high altar of the cathedral and in the centre of the western crypt. If this was the Lady Chapel before the building of the eastern crypt and Trinity Chapel then it had the place of honour in the western crypt. There are rich screens around the altar, with much heraldic decoration and the ceiling, a lierne vault, is a firmament with constellations of suns, moons and stars.

CHAPTER XI

Pilgrimage

Journeys to places of religious significance are as old as mankind. The Old Testament sets the pattern for Christians. Abraham, already past the best of life, was sent from his home to find a new land promised by God. He was a wandering Aramean, as a later saying has it, living in tents. The nomadic tradition, travelling light, continued through the wilderness years after the Exodus and God was seen as present with them not in a place set apart, fixed, but in the Tent of Presence, in the pillar of cloud and fire, providing guidance, leadership and protection.

The Jews settled in Palestine and then had a place chosen by God as the focal point of liturgy. At least they acted as if God had chosen the place. If you have some central place, a temple, then journeying there follows as naturally as day follows night. The great cycle of feasts became known as pilgrim feasts as the whole nation came together in Jerusalem to celebrate them. Of course, the whole nation didn't actually come, but a sufficiently huge crowd came that gave the feeling of a whole nation coming together.

Christianity has no such central place but in the fourth century a Spanish lady, Egeria, travelled to the Holy Land to seek out the places associated with the life and passion of Christ, and from that developed the journeying to religious centres as a part of Christian tradition. The great centres in Europe, especially after access to Jerusalem was lost in the Arab invasions, were Rome and Compostella: the shrines of SS Peter and Paul in the one, and St James in the other.

In England Canterbury and Walsingham dominated but there were a great many more, places like Hailes, now almost totally forgotten.

The medieval pilgrimage was more than just a religious journey. It combined a sense of holiday with the desire to travel, to see other places and other people. Often it was the result of a vow. King Henry III built Westminster Abbey anew in exchange for his vow to visit the Holy Land. Travel then was not only slow but considerably more dangerous: roads were mere tracks and there were wild animals to fear as well as thieves.

In the last fifty years there has been a great growth in pilgrimage.

Partly because people now have more time, leisure and money, and travel is relatively easy. Taizé, Iona, Lindisfarne, Glastonbury are among the farflung places people travel to. Those who are custodians of holy places have also made them more attractive for pilgrims, providing hospitality and making the visit of greater spiritual benefit. This is certainly the case with greater churches, whose aim at least as stated, is to turn every visitor into a pilgrim. I don't think you can become a 'pilgrim' having already arrived, but it is possible having just come because it's here and we're having a day out, that can be made a spiritual experience. So, in particular, shrines are being renewed, places for prayer set up.

A pilgrim is a stranger. That's what the roots of the word mean, and that makes an important first point. On pilgrimage we leave home. We go away from the familiar, the safe, the routine, the expected and open ourselves up to the unfamiliar. At the very least, like all travel, it takes us to places we do not know, with different people and different customs. There is a spiritual need in us to be away from the ordinary and the comfortable. However wide and deep our home life is it is still a kind of rut, a channel if you prefer, and it is good to leave that and join someone else's. In an alien environment our eyes are opened and we gain a wider experience of life. We can discover new things, but only if we go open and expectant. That isn't to say that where we go is better than home, but it is different. So it is important in going on pilgrimage that we do not make it as much like ordinary life as possible. Quite the reverse is called for. If your pilgrimage is rather like the packaged holiday in Spain that gives you Blackpool with sunshine then there's not much point. You've got to find yourself somehow a stranger.

Pilgrims travel light. I am always amazed by how much I pile into the car just for two or three days away. We need not only to make do with less possessions, but to leave behind us the baggage of everyday life which we normally carry around with us. The pressures of work, the worries we have, the responsibilities: these can be left at home.

The way is not meant to be easy. In earlier ages travel, by definition, wasn't easy but planes, trains and cars make it all too easy. Perhaps people need to build in the hardship somewhere. Some of it might be done on foot, or by cycle, especially the last bit, even if it's only crossing the causeway to Lindisfarne, or from Harbledown into Canterbury, or the traditional mile barefoot from the Slipper Chapel (that's how it got its name) to Walsingham. The hardship isn't to make you feel better, or to be done for scoring points – look, I've got more blisters than you, stuff. It may be a penance – secretly if so – but the hard way is nearly always the way to be with God, to be with others, to be closer to the earth and to the places you are travelling through. You see far more walking than you do driving. I love those walks with a group of friends where the pattern of people is constantly changing. Sometimes you are in dialogue with various individuals and sometimes part of the larger group. That's a way of deepening friendships.

Speaking of penance reminds me that penitence has often been a reason for pilgrimage: a way of saying sorry and which needs to cost us. Cain, you may remember, was set to wander the earth as a result of his killing his brother. Although going on pilgrimage is not merely to wander and the journey is at least as important as the arriving. Often we go in groups but it can be a solitary activity, and even in a group you need space for solitude and contemplation. Whether alone or with others there needs to be a willingness to engage with the unexpected, because God is waiting to reveal something. That may come on the pilgrimage journey, or at the goal of our going which Stephen Platten describes as a dazzling vision.[1] The goal calls to us, we are eager to be there. There is a yearning in us and the place has a magnetic quality. I think that has to do with its holiness. But the dazzling vision becomes central to us as we take step after step, mile upon mile. Self is displaced and the purpose, the holiness, the sense of a meeting with God takes over and becomes the inner compulsion. The vision may be of something we have heard or we have seen pictures of. I guess most pilgrims to Canterbury knew how suddenly the cathedral towers would appear in the Kentish landscape. They knew of the incredible magnificence of St Thomas' shrine. Others may have told us of the deep peace they experienced and which they want us to share. But of course the vision is not just of Bell Harry rising magnificently above Canterbury's roofs, or the island just off the coast, or Bardney afloat in the sea. It is God. Our goal and pilgrimage is always with Him, but to Him and when we arrive we shall only find peace if it is Him we are seeking in the graces that come through the holy places.

And then we must return.

Often the journey is hard and perhaps we are mad is in our thoughts.

With the voices singing in our ears, saying
That this was folly
    . . . and so we continued

And arriving at evening, not a moment too soon
Finding the place; it was (you may say) satisfactory.[2]

But if like Eliot's Magi we simply return to our places which are of the old dispensation we shall no longer be at ease. We need to allow the pilgrimage to change us.

Sometimes we may go on pilgrimage to a cathedral, but more often we will probably visit when we are on holiday, or doing a day's business or shopping. And we may have opportunity to visit our own cathedral more frequently. Our visit may be to look at the architecture, or to explore some special feature. We might go intending to look at the glass, or the tombs and memorials or we go with torch to look at misericords. These are good reasons for a visit, but they are not pilgrimages. We can, however, go on a kind of pilgrimage, to places with which we are familiar. The difference is in the intention. Are we going to look, or to meet God? I know it isn't as simple as that, for God may meet us anyway, but I am sure our visits made with a particular spiritual purpose will give us greater joy. I remember going with a friend to Durham. A close friend of my friend had died. I knew him slightly. The funeral had not been local and Jane had not been able to be there. She wanted to pray for him and so we went, with flowers, to Cuthbert's shrine, and laid the flowers there and prayed. It was an illuminating time which I treasure many years later.

Pilgrimage is a metaphor for life itself. The journey is a search for meaning and direction. It is to find our place within the natural cycles of time, and life and death. For some the path is sufficient. The exploration and the search provide enough meaning and the goal is too diffuse to be articulated. The path is often a context in which to live is to resonate with history and spirituality. The Christian life is like that. Others have trod the path before us and are still with us in the corporate memory as well as in the things they left behind: ideas, buildings, books, poems, and not least these great churches. And even if we never leave our small occupied space prayer itself is an endless pilgrimage.

I like to think of my approach to a shrine as a trysting point with my divine lover as well as with my fellow pilgrims, the saint, and the mystery of it all. All is caught up into that dazzling darkness which is the glory of God. The flowers left, the candles burnt, the prayers stumblingly said – these are tokens of love.

The Purbeck slab made for the tomb of Bishop Nigel of Ely. He died in 1169 and it shows his soul against the body of St Michael, the Archangel.

The cemetery at the Anglican Benedictine Priory at Burford.

The chantry chapel of Bishop John Stanbury, Hereford Cathedral.

CHAPTER XII

Death, Burial, Chantries

Churches are places of burial. Over the centuries the area around has been used over and over again, and we nearly always walk through gravestones and memorials as we walk into a church. Important people were buried inside the church and our greater churches have many such tombs and memorials. The worst is Westminster Abbey. Worst may seem an odd word to us, but the Abbey is so cluttered. In the aisles and transepts the marble has taken over and the whole place has become more mausoleum than church.

Death was a reality of everyday to our ancestors. That is true always, but with minimal medical care, death came suddenly and painfully. Also in small communities death touches more lives. In the medieval world the reality of judgement, of heaven and hell was deep in people's minds and hearts. Making a good death, duly shriven, was literally of vital importance. For many today death is something not to be talked about. Funerals are largely taken out of the hands of the bereaved, for everything is 'undertaken' by the funeral directors. Hence their earlier designation. Bereavement is harder to cope with and we are in danger of turning it into an illness rather than a normal part of human living. The lack of faith doesn't seem to me a cause for all this. In my parish ministry almost all bereaved people have no doubt whatever than that their loved one is 'at peace'. God only occasionally figures in the situation, but thoughts of punishment, of the fires of hell are far from people's thoughts. They are simply not believed in – rightly, perhaps, but our medieval forebears believed fervently in heaven and hell, and in practical terms, even more importantly, in purgatory.

The first thing to be said is that purgatory is not a permanent condition. It is a place of preparation for heaven. If you were in purgatory then you were not going to hell. The damned, those who died unrepentant, unshriven, went to hell. Parish church walls had paintings of the doom, or judgement, showing sometimes in graphic detail the tortures of the damned. I guess you would only risk that possibility if you didn't believe in it.

Heaven is the place of God's presence and so the place of the saints.

So, as we have already seen, the saints are those who enjoy the beatific vision of God. Those whose names are in the calendar, canonized by the popes, are not the entire roll call of heaven. Hence the Feast of All Saints, when we celebrate the lives of the unknown men and women who are in heaven. Heaven then is the final destination of the redeemed but purgatory is the place of purification, or purging.

Dorothy L. Sayers in her commentary on Dante's *Il Purgatorio* puts this with her characteristic clarity.[1] She uses the example of a valuable vase which belongs to a friend. You have dropped it in a fit of rage or through carelessness. To bring matters back to normal you must (a) be sorry and (b) be forgiven, but even then when your guilt has been admitted and you are forgiven, the vase remains broken and you are still subject to rage or carelessness. The final part, therefore is called satisfaction: reparation to your friend and amendment in yourself. So you might buy another vase for your friend and try to do something about your temper. Sin though is also against God and to make satisfaction to Him is impossible except by the redeeming graces of the death and resurrection of Jesus. However, what remains still is the stain of sin, 'the coarsening of fibre, and the clouding of the mind and imagination'.

> I waive the quantum of the sin,
> The hazard of concealing,
> But och' it hardens a'within,
> And petrifies the feeling.

Only when the clear sight and tender conscience are restored is the soul set free to stand before the unveiled light of the presence of God, which otherwise it could not endure. 'Purgatory . . . is a process of spiritual improvement which is completed precisely when it is complete.' The poem quoted is by Robert Burns, an unlikely supporter of purgatory one would have thought.

Allied to this belief in purgatory was the power of intercessions, hence the prayers for the dead to help them through this period of purgation. Pain it may have been, but cathartic, cleansing, healing.

This doctrine makes sense to me because I fear, that along with C.S. Lewis, at death I will not be ready for the unveiled light of God's presence, and with Cardinal Newman's Gerontius I will plead, 'Take me away and in the lowest depths . . .' The saints may pass indeed from this life to heaven, but most of us need the cleansing and healing.

Medieval people left instructions and gifts to ensure that their souls were prayed for, sometimes in what must seem an exaggerated way. The most elaborate means of prayer were the chantry chapels. A chapel was built, often within a church, where masses could be said for the deceased, and an endowment was made so that priests could be paid for doing this. The College of St William in York, close to the east end of the Minster, was built to house the great many chantry priests of the cathedral. The cathedral at Lincoln has three chapels which extend the walls of the Angel Quire: chantries for three bishops – Fleming who died in 1461, Russell who died in 1494, and Longland who died in 1548. They are close to the shrines of St Hugh and there are many other graves and tombs in that area. Being buried near a saint was clearly an added advantage. The retroquire of Winchester illustrates this too. Beaufort, Wayneflete, Fox and Gardiner have chantries near the shrine, with Langton and Fox elsewhere. These date from the century after 1447. Notable lay people had chantries too. One of the most famous is that of the Black Prince in Canterbury. His tomb is in the Trinity Chapel close to St Thomas' shrine, but the chantry chapel, with two altars, is in the crypt and now transformed into the Huguenot Chapel. He gazes up from his tomb chest at a painting representing the Trinity. The eyes of effigies are often open because of the words in Job: 'I shall see God and mine eyes shall behold him' (19.27).

Chantry chapels are exquisite architecture, many with carvings of great delicacy and features like miniature fan vaults. They were something that developed in the latter part of the medieval period as the doctrine of purgatory was more clearly defined. However, bishops' and abbots' tombs abound in our greater churches, and they continue, although in different styles, after the Reformation. Increasingly lay people were also buried in churches and their tombs can be of great magnificence. The guilds of medieval towns have been described as burial clubs. They saw that their members who were neither rich nor famous were properly buried and their souls prayed for.

All of this centred around the death of Jesus. His death was at the heart of the medieval religious experience. Crucifixes and prayers to Christ on the Cross were common, and this would be the representation of Christ that was uppermost in the imagination. Manuals were written to help people with their dying – *Ars Moriendi*, the craft of a good death. These books are totally centred on Christ. A crucifix would be brought by the priest when he came to anoint the body and to give the last Holy Communion The oils were for healing and the Communion was called Viaticum – food for the journey. Often the person would be laid on a piece of sackcloth sprinkled with ashes in a cross shape. The bodies of the rich and important would be dressed in death: bishops in robes, for example, but most had, at best, a simple shroud. Bodies were buried head at the west end, so that at the last judgement they would be facing east to greet the coming Christ.

Our beliefs and practices are different, but visiting great churches we can't escape graves and tombs and memorials of those who once were living as we are. John Mirke, a fifteenth-century priest, began a funeral sermon with these words: 'Good men, as yee all see, here is a mirror to us all: a corpse brought to the church.'[2] The reality of our own death cannot be ignored for ever. Most people seem to believe that the body is only a clothing for the soul which being immortal passes into eternity at the time of death. But, what then do we mean by the resurrection of the body?

We have a strong desire to be remembered, and rare indeed is the grave without a memorial stone, and our cathedrals continue to be adorned with plaques and occasionally effigies of the dead. There are modern examples of effigies on chests in the ruins at Coventry, in Boxgrove Priory and in Liverpool Cathedral. And what of the graves of saints of recent years? Edward King is a lesser festival. His grave is in the cloisters at Lincoln. Michael Ramsey, because he hasn't been dead for fifty years, is only a commemoration. His ashes are buried in Canterbury's cloister and there is a memorial on the wall nearby.

Let me end this chapter with two quotations. The first from Clarke.[3] 'It would be difficult to exaggerate the degree to which the whole of later medieval worship was dominated by the thought of the departed and particularly by the need for shortening the pains of purgatory.' That is certainly no longer true, but services of memorial, requiems, and prayers for the departed, are once more quite common.

The other quotation is from St Cyprian, Bishop of Carthage in the third century. 'Our brothers are not to be mourned for, since we know that they are not lost, but gone before; while appearing to lose they have really gained ground, as travellers and navigators are wont to do.' I like that idea of the continuing journey into God, from whom we come, in whom we live and to whom we are returning.

An aerial view of the ruined eastern arm of the Cistercian church at Rievaulx in North Yorkshire.

A rare example of a Norman Chapter House, built for the Augustinian Canons at Bristol.

Vicars' Close, reputedly the oldest inhabited street in Europe, shows the communal life of the men who sang in the Cathedral Choir at Wells.

At Hexham the night stairs survive in the south transept. The canons came down from the dormitory directly into the church for the service sung during the night.

The centre of every greater church was the Quire where the services were sung each day. This is at Chichester.

The sculpture by Stephen Broadbent in the Cloister at Chester called the Water of Life. It was placed there to mark the 900th anniversary of the founding of Chester Abbey in 1992.

The Chair of St Augustine was made in the early thirteenth century.

The throne in Norwich Cathedral, with elements dating back to the seventh century.

CHAPTER XIII

Community

All these churches, whatever their origins, were built for a Christian community for their worship. Any local church, whether parochial, collegiate or monastic is the church in that place, and all such local churches in communion with the bishop are together the Church.

Koinonia is a Greek word, often translated as fellowship, which is a fundamental concept here. It is a New Testament word, which although the apostolic writers do not equate with 'church', is the term that well expresses the mystery which underlies the various images the writers use of the Church.

Koinonia is largely a Pauline word, but it is used in Acts 2.42 where the Christians are described as following the apostolic teaching, the breaking of bread, prayer together and a 'common life' i.e. *koinonia*. 1 John also speaks of a common life and sharing in Christ's life when we walk in the light and not in darkness. St Paul tells the Corinthians that it is God 'who called you to "share" in the life of His Son, Jesus Christ' (1 Cor 1.9) and he uses the same word about the relationship with demons and idol worship. 'You can't "share" life with Christ and with anyone else.'

Koinonia then is an intimate sharing of life, living a common life, and that life lived in relationship to Jesus Christ. This is reflected in the other images for the Church: the body of Christ, the bride of Christ, the household of God.

The heart of Christian *koinonia* is in God Himself: the union with God in Christ through the Holy Spirit. This is the *koinonia* of Christian people. We are caught up into the life of the Holy Trinity and because we are all drawn into the divine life we have fellowship – *koinonia* – with one another. And it is that way round. We do not have *koinonia* of ourselves, but only from being incorporated into Christ. 'We are one body because we all share in the one bread.' Not we share in one bread and therefore are one body.

The ARCIC documents used this concept widely.[1] The Eucharist is the effectual sign of *koinonia*, episcope serves *koinonia* and primacy is a visible link and focus for it.

We can best explore the reality of *koinonia* in the different sorts of communities which created these churches in order to have a deeper understanding of what it means for us. We shall do this particularly in looking at the Rules of St Benedict and Augustine.

We might begin though by reflecting on our own communities; we all belong to several circles of community: the place in which we live, our neighbours, friends; and the kind of place will mean varying kinds of community: village, town, city. Then there is church, work, leisure. We might ask ourselves which of those have a spiritual element, and how is that expressed?

The monastic community – in which I include Benedictines, Cistercians and the Augustinian canons – those are communities of choice. A process of discernment will have taken place in which the individual and the community itself will have judged whether this is a vocation for that person. They are places in which not only worship is shared but every other aspect of life: possessions, eating, sleeping, working. So the monastery is the place shared by all.

Prebendal churches then and all modern cathedrals have a much looser common life, worship and perhaps a general way of life, but that is it. They also have layers of belonging: at the centre the dean and chapter, then the members of the foundation, singers, vergers, administrators and so on. But then many other people who see themselves as a part of the community – certainly those who live in the diocese but others far beyond, who may have a formal link through the Friends.

The smallest communities are those which share a home – the family. Social commentators tell us that it is often not parents and 2.4 children, but whatever the make-up the family Benedict has things to teach. First, listening to each other. He tells the abbot (a term which simply means father) to listen to even the youngest member of the community. Decisions are made well when each person listens hard to what the others are saying. How often we need to hear the words that aren't being said, the body language as well as the speech. The abbot's decision is accepted by all and when parents learn to earn respect and really listen, then perhaps their decisions will be accepted too. Clearly the decision-making changes as children grow, but how do couples themselves make their decisions? What are the underlying principles?

The monks eat together. Families need to share not only food but enjoy each other's company. The table is a place for sharing love. Mealtimes need space and not to be rushed if this is to happen. We nearly all live busy lives but perhaps we can set aside an evening each week, and Sunday dinnertime (whenever that is) as family time centred around a meal. Everyone can help share over time in the preparation, the serving and the clearing up.

Monks work together: jobs are shared. It is good when everyone feels they have a stake in the common enterprise, but it can't be just using the children to do the tasks you don't like.

Above all the monks pray together and I guess for many families this is the hardest part. It needs to start with couples who pray – perhaps an Office – just a reading from a Psalm or a Gospel, a while of silence, then of sharing thoughts and some time for vocal or silent prayer. When the children come, pray with them. Parents talk a great deal in ways and with words children don't understand, but if you want them to pray, to know and trust God, then begin at their beginning.

Membership of a religious community is voluntary. Members of the human family begin as fact, but the relationship of children to parents changes. Children grow into adults – that is so obviously true – but they have to change from being your children in relationship to you, to an adult-adult relationship. Of course, parents don't stop being parents, but children who are grown up need to be treated as grown up. The sibling relationships change too and new people are welcomed into the family – friends, and eventually sons and daughters-in-law. It is a changing pattern and the stronger the family is, the stronger the community, the more readily these changes can be allowed to happen without stress. Involvement in the family at some point becomes voluntary. Knowing when this point has been reached, and perhaps offering the freedom rather than reluctantly submitting to its demand, is better. Letting go is very hard but immensely important. Kids make mistakes and hurt themselves and others in the process, but we must let them do it. It's the price of maturity and aren't we glad others let us do it?

The Rule of St Benedict is a document some 73 chapters long. They are mostly short and he writes with clarity and a deep discernment of human nature. In recent years a number of books have been written about the Rule and as commentaries, so here I shall just outline the basic vows of the Benedictine way. These apply also to the Cistercians. Chapter 58 is the relevant one.

Benedict says that admission to the monastery is not to be easy. 'If the newcomer continues to knock on the door, and it is seen that he puts up patiently with the unkind replies and the difficulty of getting in', then he is to be allowed in to the guest quarters for a few days.

Then, after a further wait he may become a novice. Even in the novitiate Benedict makes it clear that the would-be monk is to have all the hardest features, the disadvantages, made very clear to him. 'And if he still holds his ground', then the next stage is permitted. The promises which the monk is called upon to make 'in the oratory, in the presence of all', are stability, conversion of life and obedience. The new monk writes, in his own hand, a petition which he places on the altar and then he sings a verse from Psalm 119 (v 116), 'Accept me, O Lord, according to your word, and I shall live, and you will not disappoint me in my hope'. The rest of the Rule makes it clear that celibacy and poverty are required but they are not vowed. St Benedict has harsh things to say about private possessions, but the community itself does not seek poverty for its own sake. A Benedictine community will have word-processors, up-to-date agricultural machinery, washing machines and so on. So, what of these three vows?

First, stability. As a Benedictine you join a particular house. There isn't some wider Order that you join and then you are allotted to a particular community. So the first aspect of stability is the place itself. This is the place, these are the people, with whom you will live and worship, work and pray for the rest of your life. This is symbolized by the enclosure. There is both an act of commitment to the community, to this group of men or women, but also a determination to put down roots. Our stability is actually in God, and the regular rhythms of life, the round of prayer, the opus Dei, the yearly cycle of festivals and fasts, all of that and much else are the roots which hold us in place. The tree draws nourishment from its roots which is why the amount of tree below ground is often at least as large as that above. The monk has to develop these unseen sources of nourishment. Stability is then about roots, about standing firm, of not wanting to run away or escape challenges. It is the vow which helps to fight envy and jealousy, those insidious thoughts that knock about in our heads which start 'if . . . ' If I was different . . . If I was there and not here . . . We can find God where we are. He is here and this is where he has placed us. This is the soil in which he wants us to grow, to blossom and to flourish. Constant changes make us dissatisfied and create drift and unhappiness. So we can ask ourselves about the things which are roots for us. Prayer, our church community (how committed are we to them? Not just to St Mary's, but to Mary and Josh and Freda and Mick?), the people, music, books. I think the church building can be a place of deep rootedness for us, for over the years it is not only the place of regular prayer, but also of great joys in baptisms, weddings, celebrations, of sorrows too. We come to the same place for funerals, and when our hearts are heavy and we don't know which way to turn. The familiar and the loved, the memories it has for us, can be a real balm. Much as our homes themselves can be.

The second vow is 'conversion of life'. All the commentators say that Benedict's Latin words are all but impossible to translate, but the gist is clear. If stability is about roots and standing firm, then conversion is about change, about growth. The monk is not set in a dull routine that is to be unchanging. He is seeking for God and that search brings changes to us. Most of the people I know who either are monks and nuns, or have been novices, have found the experience deeply disturbing. The change has come at the profoundest levels. The jargon speaks of monastic formation, but it seems that before that can happen there has to be a de-formation. Entering into new experience will have elements of that but the commitment to grow, to develop, to undergo painful change, is another area of our lives which it will be profitable to explore. But it is a bit more complicated than that, because not only are you changing, growing, but so are the others. The pattern of interpersonal activity is therefore also in a state of constant flux. And there we see again the value of stability. The roots of the little oak trees in Norfolk enable the branches to withstand the strong winds off the North Sea. Our stability enables us to hold fast when the changes come at us like a gale, or worse.

The third vow is obedience. Almost everyone thinks that the word means doing as we are told: that it's about giving or receiving commands. If it is, then it has become thin and weakens community life. The word's roots are in listening. So I repeat something of what I have said earlier about our need to listen to each other. To really try to hear what is being said, and then trying to make as positive a response as possible. Obeying is not doing as you are told, baldly, but listening to God in all that is going on and then answering Yes. If you are the one in authority and you know you will be obeyed, then you have to be even more careful of what you ask. Benedict also emphasizes the fact that the abbot, who is not an autocrat but a loving father, is himself under obedience, to the Rule and, of course to the Gospel. In the end the question to answer is: how in these circumstances can I respond in the most Gospel-like manner?

The Benedictine community is seen as a family of brothers with their father, but as communities grew in size it became necessary for there to be smaller units within the community and other officers. The Rule deals with some of the problems that can arise with the appointment of officers but the most salient feature is that the abbot remains responsible for everything, under God.

The quire and the chapter house are the places you can most easily see today how the Benedictine family works. In the quire each person has his space allotted to him. Everyone has his part to play in the opus Dei. In the chapter house the seats are arranged around the walls. Everyone's opinion is to be heard, and the building encourages participation – there are no back rows. I am sure Parochial Church Councils should sit in this way. Within the seniority of admission there is a great deal of equality. As in any family, Benedictine reserves enough structure and authority to make the place function, but otherwise leaves a great deal of freedom.

Quire and chapter house, but also many other places around the cloister and beyond, are the places of the monk's life: bakehouse, storerooms, gardens, library, infirmary, guesthouse, gatehouse. There are also many tasks to be done, if the community is to function. The monastery is an ordered place. When we visit the monasteries that are now ruined, we perhaps think of them as solitary, quiet, sleepy places, but although a great deal of silence would be practised they were, and are, busy places. No-one rushing around, but each person doing the tasks, the work allotted to him, and as a bell rings, the immediate moving from one task to another: from cloister or brewery to church, and then when the service is done, no lingering, but on to the next task. The day is full, but also varied: prayer, worship, study, administration, household chores, gardening, writing – a balanced life. Most of us have a great deal to learn from that. An exercise you might like to try is to take a day and ask yourself what you are doing each hour on the hour. For a great many people there will be stretches of a single activity for too long a period. Recognizing that is one thing, but implementing change is another.

The Cistercians grew out of the Benedictine communities. Reform began at a place called Cîteaux in Burgundy about 1098. A group of monks left their monastery so that they could live more exactly according to the Rule. They wanted to keep more to the letter, to live a much simpler life. This was a reaction against an earlier change. Based on the practises of the monastery at Cluny there had come into existence a large group of houses known as Cluniacs. They were still Benedictines but the way they developed the liturgy meant that manual work was edged out of their life. Increasingly they spent almost all their waking hours in church. The men who went to Cîteaux and to the communities which spread all across Europe decided to return to the balance of Benedict's Rule: a simpler liturgy, just as Benedict prescribed, study, reading, manual work. They believed that because so many abbeys were in towns, and therefore attracted visitors in large numbers, this distracted from their principle work of prayer. Monasteries were indeed schools, hospitals, guesthouses and visited not just by ordinary travellers but by important people. Kings and their officers, bishops and others came and were often a drain on their financial resources as much as deflecting them from their con-templative lives. Cistercians therefore built their abbeys in remote, inaccessible places. The sites of the ruins like Roche and Rievaulx make this clear even today. The Cistercian house was a total enclosure. Life was austere, simple, direct. They were very much withdrawn from the world. One other thing makes the Cistercians distinct. In addition to the choir monks there were lay brothers. These lived in an almost separate community centred on the west side of the cloister. They used the nave of the church for their simpler offices, and they did the larger share of the hard graft. The choir monks did their share, but the larger part of prayer was theirs, the larger part of the manual work the lay brothers. We see these beautiful ruins but it was, and is, a hard life indeed. But what can we learn from these communities?

First, I think we can pick up some clues about balance in our lives. Not just the idea of different sorts of activities and not allowing one element to dominate, to the exclusion of all else, but with the balance, what proportion of the various activities. That we have a problem here may have been exposed by the exercise above. For most working people, our paid employment will take the largest share, but we may decide that the time has come to do paid work part-time so that we can do some voluntary work, or so that we can help care for grandchildren. If you are a busy wife and mother, having a part-time job, even with a 'modern' husband, home and family will take the lion's share, but we must find time for ourselves.

Cistercians can also help us to see that life can be lived more simply than we do. Perhaps we don't need all these possessions? What about our diet? Could that be simpler, cheaper, healthier? How much of our resources do we share with others, either through hospitality or by giving things and money away?

Lastly, I would point to the combination of being withdrawn and contemplative. You may be certain you are not called to be a contemplative monk or nun if you are reading this, but contemplation is a way of looking at things as well as a way of praying. We can all participate in that. Contemplation is to look at things, at life, just looking, lingering, not so much observing as becoming attached with passion: seeing things subjectively and with what Bishop Holloway calls the 'involvement of the lover watching the beloved'. Our horizons are widened when we do this. Tiny things gain in significance, and the world becomes deeper and so much the richer. It is the way of poets, of storytellers, of musicians, of lovers. And our ability to see contemplatively will come the more we seek to do it. Which is where withdrawal will help. To take some time and space away from the normal everyday, and to seek in that space and silence to look and look, and listen, and to be, that is the path to contemplation. We may do it for an hour or two: I think of Annie Dillard at her creek, sitting on its banks or on a bridge.[2] We may engage in this in an art gallery, or, I hope, in the spaces of our great churches. But the important thing is to come away, just as Jesus so often did. The Gospel exemplar is Mary of Bethany and you will recall Jesus' response to her sister, Martha, when she, worried and fretful, wanted her sister to help. 'Only one thing is necessary,' says Jesus. We all need to let go of the worries and distractions of our lives and simply be with Jesus (Luke 10.38f). The Cistercian spends time singing the Offices and in private prayer, but the contemplative life is all – just as much as when engaged in milking the cows, or setting up the pottery kiln for a firing, or ploughing a field. Our little withdrawals will make a difference to our living too. The churches are important in our rushed, self-centred world, as signs and symbols of the contemplative.

The regular canons were so-called because they followed a rule, in distinction from those whose lives were ordered by statutes or no particular system. The regular canons were not monks although theirs was a semi-monastic life, but unlike the Benedictines they were priests. I do not mean that Benedictines weren't, or aren't priests, but Benedict himself was not and the ethos of Benedictinism is lay. The Rule has some searching comments about clergy who want to be monks. The regular canons saw their ministry, their communal life in priestly terms, although they also had a lot in common with the Benedictines. The chief distinction, other than being priestly, was that of having no enclosure. The canons were outward looking. The Rule that many of these communities, founded in the early decades of the twelfth century, observed was that of St Augustine. To find its origins we must turn to the fourth century and to North Africa.

Augustine was the Bishop of Hippo and one of the great thinkers and writers of his day. He wrote the Rule, a short, but rather generalized document, about 397 for the community he had established in his episcopal residence in Hippo. Like many similar rules it had had a period of gestation. There had been an earlier foundation in 388 at Tagaste, only a year after Augustine's baptism, and there are many parallels and comments on the Rule in Augustine's sermons and letters. The Rule was copied widely in Gaul, Spain and Italy but only after the ninth century did it form the basis for definite groups of men and women, and then in the eleventh century it 'spread like fire through stubble'.[3]

Augustine's inspiration was the first community of Christians in Jerusalem which is recorded in Acts 4.32-3. 'The whole group of believers was united, heart and soul; no-one claimed for his own anything that he had, as everything they owned was held in common. The apostles continued to testify to the resurrection of the Lord Jesus with great power, and they were all given great respect.'

Those sharing in this life were to 'be of mind and one heart'(1.2) This unity is to come first from simplicity of living. A detachment from the stream of temporal things, the leaving aside the things which pass away in order to create a group of people each of whom has a deep, inner unity. In his commentary on Ps 133 Augustine wrote: 'We live in unity in such a way that we form one person. Many bodies but not many hearts.' The community's life is the practical outworking of love. 'Only those in whom love for Christ is perfect truly live together in unity.'

No matter the social or educational background, everyone came into the community on an equal footing. And the purpose of this life is summed up in this quotation from Augustine: 'Together one, in the one Christ, on the way to the one Father.' Seeing life as a journey towards God marks out the essentially religious note of the communities and gives it a sense of the dynamic. Augustine's Rule is more about a movement than creating the structures of an institution. In this way it is a great contrast to Benedict. Augustine's canons are not just to pray together, eat and sleep together but to share an inner life which was not focussed on themselves but on others. The recently installed Dean of Bristol referred to the regular canons' ways in his address on that occasion. He spoke of the things they wanted to do and quoted their words: 'They wanted to suffer weakness with the weak, and distress with the fallen. They wanted to be light in a dark place. Their treasure was to be in the cure of souls not in endowments.'[4] The Gospel pattern for them was again to be that of Mary and Martha. Martha was to be an inspiration too, as she busied herself with people's needs. Theirs was to be a ministry which united the contemplative and the practical. Interestingly, the Dean sees their inspiration as a way of inspiring the cathedral, which had been founded for Augustinian canons, in its work now. Perhaps others elsewhere might find a renewed enthusiasm and inspiration by exploring the roots from which their communities have grown. It takes imagination and sensitivity, and a careful reading of our own times. But to return to Augustine.

The Jerusalem community had no individual possessions but owned all things in common, and this was to be true in Augustine's Rule. For him this is not so much an economic as a spiritual matter. It is about simplicity rather than poverty and a recognition that others own what I have, and I own, in others, what I do not have. This too is undergirded by the love which respects the needs, the gifts, the characters of each person.

Augustine goes on to write about worship, yet unlike Benedict does not lay out a pattern, but goes deeper. The words of the Liturgy are to be alive in their hearts (2.3) but Benedict will echo Augustine's demand that the place of prayer is kept solely for that purpose. Deans and Chapters, please listen to this. The canons' work was to involve the care of the sick and those in need. It was to be a social protest. A community of love over against a society dominated by possessiveness, pride and power. That was true of the Church in Roman North Africa, of the Augustinian canons of the twelfth century, and for us today.

Christians today can create communities which challenge the accepted social order. We can look at our own lives and discover how much in the way we live comes from the Gospel and how much is of the society in which we live. How simple is our living? What importance does prayer have in our lives? Are we more concerned about the others around us than about ourselves? Do we have a concern for the weak and the fallen? Do we see ourselves as on the way to God? What are our aims, our intentions? Is it about gaining possessions, new car, bigger house, expensive clothes and holidays, or are we genuinely concerned about our neighbours? Love is the key word, a deep, passionate love for others, reflecting God's prior love for us. Of our local Christian community, can it be said to be together, in the one Christ, on the way to the Father? And what can we do to make that more so?

Augustine's Rule as we have seen was originally devised for his own episcopal household. Another bishop, Chrodegang of Metz also wrote a rule for his household. They, however, lived less of their life in common. Obviously worship, but they had their own houses and retained their own money and had an individual income – a stipend. That word is still used for the payments to the clergy. It is not a wage or salary earned, but enough to live on, so that you can be free to engage in whatever tasks come your way without having to worry about money. Stipends set you free, at least in theory, but the modern priest, usually married and with family, has different needs and his family may have different aspirations. But the desire to bring the clergy serving a particular church to live together was strong. Communal life gives mutual support, helps alleviate some of the stresses of celibacy, and makes for an example of Christian living. The Lateran Synod of 1059 exhorted cathedral clergy to live together and many adopted the Rule of St Augustine, but in many places across Europe a different pattern grew up more akin to the arrangements created by Chrodegang. The prebendal system was to be found in Chichester, Exeter, Hereford, Lichfield, Lincoln, Salisbury, Wells and York. There were some communal funds, but each prebend had his own income, lived in his own house and was only bound by the vows of ordination and the cathedral's statutes. Many of the prebends held prebends in many different places and were therefore absentees. Only rarely can most of the stalls in the cathedral choir have been occupied.

The basic requirement of the clergy, now as then, is to recite the daily office and clearly this is a communal activity. And that celebration together, even when as now the Office is only a twice-a-day event, requires a degree of commitment often vitiated by the distances apart the clergy live. It seems to me that if the cathedral clergy do not pray together day by day something very important is lost from the community.

Many cathedrals are currently in the process of revising their statutes. June Osborne, one of the staff at Salisbury, has written about this. 'In rewriting statutes we have to ask ourselves by what principles and ordered rules do we live in community . . . the main concern is still about the relationship of our values, symbols and structures, about how a community is held together.'[5]

These are questions we may ask of ourselves as a family, a parish church, or any community of which we are part. T.S. Eliot wrote:

> What life have you if you have not life together?
> There is no life that is not in community,
> And no community not lived in praise of God.[6]

The physical presence of churches is our starting point. How can our greater churches reveal to those who visit that these are places of community? I am sure we can learn both from Benedict and Augustine.

Richard Giles reminds us that the entrance of our churches derive their name from the hearth. Hearths are places of gathering, and he says 'Jesus is to be the hearth of our lives around whom we gather.'[7] Sometimes in our efforts to make our churches more homely we introduce easy chairs, carpets, lamps: but this rarely seems to work, for it turns the church into a private place. Churches need to be obviously public places if they are not to be clubs into which those who do not belong are able to enter freely. How can we retain a sense of being the home of a community and yet at the same time an open place for all?

The community that lives in praise of God will be an expression of a kind of living that is open boundaried. The centre needs to be strong, but the edges open and unclear. And this worship gives us a vision of the Communion of Saints – that community of the end of time when all humanity is drawn into the praise of God.

Much of modern society does not believe either of those suppositions: either that we ought to live in relationship to each other or that communities only become true communities (*koinonia*) in relationship with God. Real community is lost in many places. As it used to be said, we can only be brothers and sisters when we recognize the fatherhood of God. But the Church is precisely a community which does live to praise God. Isn't that the source of all that community is about? Worship must lead us into the unity of purpose which Augustine saw, and recognize that our journey to God isn't just about the 'religious' but about every aspect of life. Worship and the search for justice and peace are not to be unravelled. So this provides the Church with an enormous task: to be, and to be seen to be, a thriving, loving, united community, in which our concerns are for each other and for those beyond. By our living we can show the way that society can once again learn to live in communities which live in praise of God.

CHAPTER XIV

Cloisters and Gardens

In this chapter and the next we will explore two further aspects of these greater churches which express their communal nature: first, cloisters, then precincts.

'And the Lord God planted a garden in Eden, in the east' (Gen 2.8). But more of that later on. The cloister, its name derived from the Latin for shut in, was at the centre of every monastic community, but a good number of greater churches of the prebendal model also have cloisters. They are usually square with four covered paths running around the four sides. The middle is occupied by a garden.

The cloister was rather like a high street in that it was the path between all the different parts of the monastery. Cloisters are most often built to the south side of the church, for obvious reasons in the British climate, but even so at least four are to the north. The side next to the church was used for work. Often books were stored there or nearby. St Bernard said that a cloister without books was like a monastery without monks. To the east side is the chapter house, a place of daily meeting, of discussion and decision making. Of that more later. Above, on that side, was the dormitory, which had a staircase into the cloister and another into the south transept of the church. That night-stair survives in part at Bristol and, magnificently at Hexham. Then on the south side was the refectory – the place where monks or canons ate together, and nearby, of course, the kitchen. One of the distinctions of the Cistercian houses was the position of the refectory. Theirs are normally sited on the same side as others but at right angles. The very splendid hall can still be seen at Rievaulx, a very large building. The refectory at Chester is off the north side of the north-placed cloister, and is still in use as a refectory, although now for the public. The main difference is that the noise of knives and forks has conversation added, whereas the monks would have been silent, whilst someone read to them. This remains the practice in monastic houses. Chester has a superb pulpit for the reader to use and part of one survives at Hexham although now placed in the presbytery.

The fourth side, the west, was the cellarer's department, according to the Rule 'He is to have care of everything'. The west range therefore is a store place for all sorts of things. Benedict says that everything is to be treated with care. 'All the monastery's utensils and goods he should regard as if sacred altar vessels. He should studiously avoid both miserliness and extravagant squandering of the monastery's resources. All things are to be done in moderation (31.3 and 10). In some cathedrals these buildings are open to the public, used as display areas, museums and libraries.

This brief survey makes clear that the cloister was, and is, a place of coming and going. Silently, though. The life of a monastery was largely silent. The arrangement of places around the cloister shows the balance of life which the medieval world sought to create. The monk or canon moved from task to task when a bell sounded in order to create a balance between prayer, work, rest. We can ask ourselves questions about balance in our own lives. How do we divide our time? Do we work too hard, or not enough? Do we spend time with our friends and families? What about holidays? Do we make time for God? For prayer, and meditation?

To us the cloister seems a place of rest, a breathing place, probably, because not all visitors find them, they were places of activity.

In the centre may well be some kind of garden. This in itself is a place of rest, a place of quiet and beauty. Come for a moment to Chester. The glass in the windows around the cloister has figures of the saints in the 1928 Prayer Book Calendar: some interesting characters there. You can walk into the centre. In the middle is a deep square pond with a tiled edge. The water is about 5 feet down. In the midst of this pond is a piece of sculpture by Stephen Broadbent. It consists of two figures: Christ and the women He met at the well of Samaria. They both hold a bowl, water pours through the bowl, drops off Christ's elbows and across His lap, and down into the pool. On the bowl are the words 'The living water' (John 4.10) in Greek, and around the square base, made in bronze, there is also an inscription from St John's Gospel 4.14. On the north side a flight of steps leads down into the water. There was also a duck on the day I was there. Around is a lawn and the edges have shrubs like hawthorn and azalea. It is a lovely place, peaceful and gentle with the sound of running water. One of the benches has the famous lines about gardens:

> The kiss of the sun for pardon,
> The song of the birds for mirth
> One is nearer God's heart in a garden
> Than anywhere else on earth.

Dorothy Gurney's words are true for a great many people, but are no excuse for not going to church.

Recent years have shown how many people find spiritual meaning in gardens. In a recent book, *Sacred Gardens*, Roni Jay says that all gardens are sacred spaces. In conversation with Guy Ogilvy and published in *The Times* review of her book on 4 April 1998 she says:

> As with any art form, when you explore and analyse it, it informs us about the history and the cultural values of a people and their relationship with place. The Persians, for example, modelled their gardens on the description of paradise in the Koran, and they planted them with trees and flowers with symbolic spiritual values such as the rose. But the idea behind the most important feature of their gardens pre-dates Islam by centuries. Back to the Book of Genesis and the Garden of Eden.

'And the Lord God planted a garden in Eden.' Incidentally, the word paradise is Persian for garden. The cloister, at Chichester, an oddly shaped one and largely used for burial in the past, is known as Paradise. Eden means delight. Isaiah looking ahead to years of restoration says that the Lord 'will make her wilderness like Eden, her desert like the garden of the Lord; joy and gladness will be found in her, thanksgiving and the voice of song' (51.3). This image of joy and song as one of God's redemption was clearly in the minds of those who created medieval gardens, but they had very practical uses too. A few medieval gardens have been investigated by archaeologists, notably the cloisters at Glastonbury which had a stone-kerbed path surrounding a small area of finely worked soil, presumably a flower bed. The cloister at Polsloe Priory in Devon was 10m x 30m and the one at Orford in Lincolnshire – a house of regular canonesses – was 20m square and boarded on three sides by a broad ditch. The fourth side sloped down to a stream. Water was for irrigation as well as for fish.

Communities actually had several gardens, of different kinds, so the cloister is only one of many. Firstly there were the herbers, gardens mainly fairly small, which were private places for refreshment, with lawns and herbaceous borders. Please note the connection between those two words: herber and herbaceous. Abbots and priors had these sorts of gardens and the cloister was probably a herber too. Other officers of the monastery or community had their own gardens as well. At Canterbury there is evidence of a small garden of Prior Wilbert's which may well have grown poisonous narcotics: mandrake, hemlock, henbane and opium poppies: for medicinal uses. The novels about Cadfael by Ellis Peters have made us familiar with the herb gardens associated with the Infirmary. This area of the community (the ruins at Canterbury can be walked through) was a small community in itself. Not only the sick and the very old were cared for there. Blood-letting was considered good for health and administered up to six times a year and the brethren spent a few days there recovering. Many of the plants grown had special uses. Bay, holly and ivy are still used for decorations at Christmas; yew and hazel catkins for the palms of Palm Sunday. You couldn't ring up some supplier to get real palm leaves through the post. Roses and sweet woodruff were used to decorate churches at Corpus Christi – often early in June. White flowers were for saints, red for martyrs.

Flowers have always been associated with St Alban for Bede tells us that the hill up which he was taken to be killed was covered with them. The modern embroidered covering of his shrine has English flowers. In Chichester Cathedral a window of St John Baptist by Christopher Webb shows him surrounded by a garland of flowers said to be blooming in Sussex on his feast day – June 24th.

The cellarer's garden had vegetables and herbs. Hay was cut for latrines and to strew on floors, together with rushes and mints. We know that they grew brassicas, leeks, parsnips, turnips and skirrets, beans and peas, garlic, chives, onions. Communities also had orchards for fruit: mulberries, medlars, quince, chestnut, walnut, apple, pear and cherry were all common. A few places had vineyards. Domesday Book of 1085 records thirty-eight of them, but by Henry II's reign in the twelfth century wine could be imported fairly cheaply from Gascony and Bourdeaux, but vines continued to grow for shade. The principle drink was beer, and the buildings of the community would include a brewery as well as granary and bakery. Fish and birds were also eaten but meat, according to St Benedict, was only for the very young, the very old and the sick. A number of houses had a meat kitchen to keep the rest of the food free of meat. The burial ground was planted with trees like an orchard.

The different sorts of communities had different kinds of gardens, depending on their work. The Cistercians had to feed themselves entirely, and are well known for their radical agrarian policies. They reclaimed land, provided by means of drainage, and they became skilled in the management of water and woodland.

The Augustinians developed a ministry to the sick as the Benedictines always had, so the various medicinal herbs were important to them.

Green has become associated with environmental concerns, but it has always had a place in theological thinking. It represents rebirth and everlasting life. Hugh of Fouilloy said, 'It is truly the nature of the colour green that it nourishes the eyes and preserves their vision.'

Gardens, parks, trees, plants, flowers become more important to us all especially when we live in cities. But to have our own garden, and to recognize it as a place of spiritual nourishment can be very creative in our lives.

A few cathedrals are doing something with their garden spaces. The small cloister at Christ Church in Oxford is a flowery mead: grass with wild flowers. At Lincoln the cloister has beds of flower associated with the Blessed Virgin Mary, although they don't strike you as exciting, it has to be said. There is an historical reconstruction near Shrewsbury Abbey, due to the fame Cadfael has brought to the abbey there. I am hesitant to mention a garden at Winchester, because if too many people discover it, it will lose its character. But if you search for it, you'll find. That is probably true too of the Bishop's Palace garden in Chichester which is open to the public and now cared for by the local council. Salisbury has some famous cedars which are rather splendid, and, with difficulty, from that cloister you can see the spire. There are often good and unusual views of towers and spires. Nearly every greater church has a great area of closely mown lawn. Please, could some of these become places for wild flowers? Surely there are people who would gladly look after a cathedral garden, if asked?

Cecil Collins designed an altar frontal for St Clement's Chapel in Chichester. It is entitled The Icon of Divine Light. That is an expression of Paradise conceived as a garden or the empyrean. And that thought leads us to Dante, whose vision of Paradise is the rose. Many of our churches have rose windows and shouldn't roses grow around them too? Plants, flowers, leaves are there in abundance in the carvings of our cathedrals. The most famous are the leaves at Southwell, in the Chapter House, but they are everywhere as well. We just need a gentle prod to remind us that particular flowers have symbolic meanings, and that they are all reminders that God is the creator and we should take delight in His creation, a creation in which evidently we share (think of an untended garden for a moment), and that gardens are always symbols of heaven – the garden of heaven, the garden of the Resurrection. We cut foliage and flowers to arrange within, so why not gardens without?

I have majored, as they say, on gardens in this look at the cloister, but you will recall that in addition to being a garden and a pathway around the buildings, it was also a place of work – and study: the reading of books, and the writing of books, and the work of illumination. The monastic work of this kind was directed towards the glory of God, and much else was done for the good of the community and those who came as guests. Love of God and love of neighbour was there, and so we might sit in a cloister, enjoy its peace and ponder our own work. Is it just to earn money? How does it give glory to God? How does it help my neighbour?

Perhaps too we might ponder the breathing spaces in our lives. How can they be bettered and are we grateful for them?

CHAPTER XV

Precincts

The great churches tower above the rooftops, dominating the skyline. Often as you come closer you discover they are hidden away from the main streets of the city. The approach may be through a great gateway, itself imposing and giving hints of what is to come. Exchequer Gate at Lincoln or the one at Canterbury, for example. This latter now has a modern welcoming Christ to greet the visitor. Often the cathedral precincts are like a separate community, another world, apart from the city, cut off by walls, by rivers. The word 'close' conveys something private and, therefore, superior, and intensified by the notices 'By order of the Dean and Chapter' kind, and the usually rather splendid buildings – medieval or Georgian.

To walk from the High Street into the Close at Salisbury is to leave the secular bustle for a place of order and tranquillity. The same feelings are aroused at Wells and even at Durham, but the air speaks of privilege too: public schools, seats of learning (Oxford and Durham), firms of august, expensive lawyers (Norwich), a cultured, 'cloistered' lifestyle.

I spent a couple of years living in a cathedral close, teaching in a choir school, and I can vouch that life there is not particularly privileged and can be as inward looking, as 'parochial' as any rural community. Except of course that everything exists for the huge building on which all is literally centred.

The close is only a place of quiet and reflective solitude for those who visit; for others it is a place of work with all the attendant stresses of modern life and only as peaceful as the inner spirit of those who live there.

To explore these apparent havens is difficult for there are signs saying 'private' and they mean that. The American visitor who has ignored the sign, enquiring if this is a real school, is not welcome in the midst of teaching real boys. But part of the charm and interest is peering through gateways, and round corners and having rather romantic notions of what it's like to live behind a door marked 'Sacrist'.

At Ely the precincts are known as the College, which was the title given to his new foundation by Henry VIII: 'The King's New College at

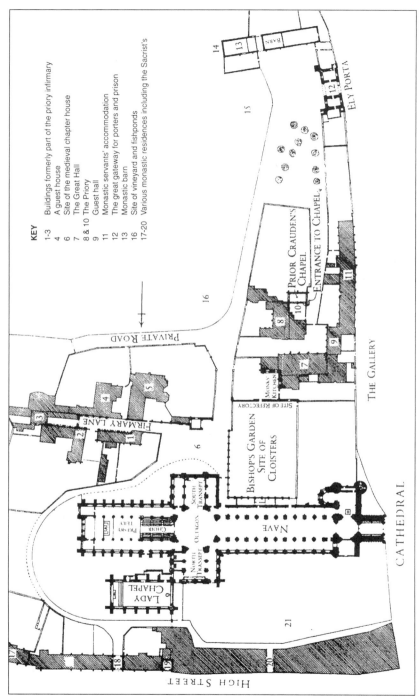

KEY

1-3	Buildings formerly part of the priory infirmary
4	A guest house
6	Site of the medieval chapter house
7	The Great Hall
8 & 10	The Priory
9	Guest hall
11	Monastic servants' accommodation
12	The great gateway for porters and prison
13	Monastic barn
16	Site of vineyard and fishponds
17-20	Various monastic residences including the Sacrist's

Plan of the Monastic Buildings in the College at Ely.

Ely'. The locally produced leaflet (undated) says that this is probably the largest collection of monastic buildings in daily use. I suppose they mean buildings not used by monks. A great many are now used by the King's School. The entrance is the Porta, the porter's lodge and prison.

> At the gate of the monastery a wise old man is to be posted, one capable of receiving a message and giving a reply, and whose maturity guarantees that he will not wander round. This doorkeeper should have a cell near the gate, so that persons who arrive may always find someone at hand to give them a reply. As soon as anyone knocks, or a poor man calls out, he should answer 'Thanks be to God' or 'God bless you.' Then with all the gentleness that comes from fear of God, he should speedily and with the warmth of charity attend to the enquirer. (RB 66.1-4)

To the right is the school dining hall made from buildings once used as barn, granary and stables. The park includes the motte of a twelfth century castle and the sites of vineyard and fishponds. 'If it is possible, the monastery should be organised so that all its needs, that is to say such things as water, a mill, a garden, and various crafts, may be met within its premises' (RB 66.6-7). The various buildings are still here: brewery, malting house, goldsmith's workshop.

To the south-east of the cathedral is a small street called Firmary Lane. These are basically Norman buildings and the street was roofed over originally and formed the main hall of the infirmary. 'The care of the sick must be seen to before and above everything else, so that they may truly be served as Christ Himself (RB 36.1). 'They are to be borne with patiently but not make excessive demands on their brethren. The man in charge is to be God-fearing, attentive and painstaking' (RB 36.7). Baths were allowed and meat 'to build up their strength' (36.9). As ever St Benedict writes out of experience. Caring for the sick is demanding, practical and often messy. Bloodletting was a frequent occurrence, even for the well, and this happened in what is now Powcher's Hall. The Black Hostelry was a place for visiting monks and a number of the officers of the monastery had houses hereabouts: cellarer, precentor and infirmarian.

The former Great Hall was at one time the Deanery, but now houses the Bishop, and the Queen's Hall, built to provide accommodation for special guests like Queen Philippa, after whom it is named (she was the wife of Edward III), together with the brewery, is now the Headmaster's House. Nearby is Prior Crauden's Chapel which is often open, but the rest of the Priory is now part of the school.

Adaption is the key word here. Buildings are treasured for being ancient, however are not simply preserved but brought into modern use and changed as required. I am sure Benedict would approve even if he wished Ely was still a monastery.

Change and adaption can be seen around the secular cathedrals too: for houses have been rebuild and restyled over the centuries. Often with medieval innards, they have been altered by Georgians and Victorians, and now often sub-divided into flats.

Originally the houses of canons were a matter of private enterprise but slowly as the years passed common ownership became the norm: at Lincoln, certainly from the end of the thirteenth century. It hadn't made sense for someone appointed to be Precentor then to have to try to find himself a house. The houses of the Dean and Chapter still surround the cathedral, but the Chancellor is the only one still to live on the same site since 1321. A charter addressed to Antony Bek, who was Chancellor then, says that he needs a 'spacious place for recreation and pleasure, and for the full duties of continuous residence, reading and preaching the holy scriptures, much study and various other duties'.[1] Before that they lived next door to the Deanery which was to the north of the cloisters, a building now part of the Minster School. The Vicars Choral lived in the square off the south side of the precincts, the Poor Clerks and choristers on the east side of Minster Yard at what is now 4, 5 and 5a, and 10. There were also residences for chantry priests: the Cantilupe Chantry founded in 1366, the house being opposite the south-east doors of the Angel Quire, and the Burghersh Chantry in James Street. The Precentory was the house just inside Exchequer Gate but its present facade gives no idea of its age. All the officers, with the exception of the Chancellor, have moved several times in recent years.

So we see various patterns of community life; the prebendal communities living quite independently of one another and only worshipping together, although with communal living for some groups like chantry priests and choristers. The monastic and regular canons lived communal lives but their buildings have either been destroyed or adapted to modern uses. Again we may find opportunity to ponder how much we live in relation to others and especially about those who live near us. What links do we have with our neighbours? Do we have any non-worship links with our fellow worshippers? And what of those we work with? Could we find a way of integrating the various groups and communities of which we are part?

116

CHAPTER XVI

Kings and Queens

The pagan kings of Anglo-Saxon kingdoms were the prime targets of the missionaries sent from Rome by St Gregory the Great at the end of the sixth century. Ethelbert of Kent already had a Christian Queen, Bertha from France, and a marriage from the Kentish royal family helped with the conversion of Edwin of Northumbria. Later, after Edwin's death and the collapse of that first mission in the north, King Oswald brought Aidan from Iona to reconvert his kingdom. King and bishop travelled together, the King acting as interpreter until Aidan learnt sufficient Anglo-Saxon.

It is inevitable that ruler and bishop should be significant for one another, either as partners, or opponents, but more often in some uneasy alliance. The Church sometimes giving credence to less than Christian regimes and the Crown sometimes usurping ecclesiastical authority.

Westminster Abbey has a unique role in the life of the nation. Edward Confessor probably refound a Benedictine monastery close to his palace of Westminster. It was the first Romanesque church in England and we catch an intriguing glimpse of it on the Bayeux Tapestry. Two centuries on Henry III rebuilt the abbey, for not only did it have royal patronage, and was to become the place of royal burial, but it housed the shrine of its founder, canonized in 1161, and was the coronation church: and all this set in the context of a Benedictine abbey. Henry III's rebuilding had strong political reasons too. His desire was to establish the Plantaganet dynasty and to envelop it with the authority of St Edward. Westminster mirrors in England the Saint Chappelle in Paris begun five years before. Henry had vowed to go to the Holy Land but used the rebuilding as a substitute. Edward was seen then as the perfect Christian ruler, and to boot he was English.

Other greater churches had royal founders, among them Cenwalh at Winchester and Cynegils at Dorchester. The fifteenth-century historian of the cathedral in Winchester, Thomas Rudborne, wrote of a modest chapel outside the north door of the nave in the place where St Swithun had originally been buried. The excavations of the Biddles in the 1960s unearthed its foundations. It seems that after Swithun's translation into the new shrine a new westwork was built with a series of important tombs set in rows around where the saint's grave had been. Tatton Brown says these are of later kings of Wessex and England including Cnut (d. 1035) and possibly Alfred.[1] The bones of these royals are now in caskets set around the presbytery screen in the cathedral.

Only one greater church is the place of coronation but statues and coloured glass images of kings are everywhere. Is this simply because England has kings? Well, yes, but there is more to it.

It was Christmas Day 1066 when William, the Duke of Normandy, was crowned in the church recently built by his predecessor. William regarded Harold as a usurper and was claiming Edward's crown. He had won it at Hastings but the ceremony of coronation would legitimate it. Where else should he be crowned than in Edward's church? In order to assert continuity with a longer tradition too, he was also crowned in Winchester.

The last coronation is now a couple of generations back so I will give a briefish outline of it. At the beginning all the regalia is carried in procession, is presented to the Archbishop of Canterbury and he lays each part on the high altar. That sets the tone: this is a religious rather than a political rite, although clearly its political focus is strong. The first part is the Recognition of the People. The archbishop asks whether the people are willing to do homage and service to the sovereign. 'God save the king' is the reply. This is not an election, but an acceptance that this is the person, and an acknowledgement that sovereignty resides in that person. The King then takes the Oath promising to govern according to law and custom, to uphold justice and mercy and to protect the Church. The point is made that the monarch is not to be an irresponsible despot but a ruler with duties towards his people. Since the coronation of William and Mary in 1689 this has been followed by the presentation of a Bible, the assumption being that James II, who had fled in what is known as the Glorious Revolution, had not ruled according to this book. The service then continues with Epistle, Gradual, Gospel and Nicene Creed, as at any Eucharist. Then comes the anointing, one of the most significant parts of the rite. That this continued through the Reformation, when all other anointings fell into disuse, reflects this. Since the coronation of George II the choir has sung Handel's anthem 'Zadok the priest' at this point. The words say that Zadok and Nathan anointed Solomon king (1 Kings 1.31f). The prophet Samuel had anointed first Saul and then David as kings, to be God's chosen. That is the significance of anointing. Old Testament kings were supposed to act as God's viceregent, and it is this idea which had been picked up in England probably as early as the ninth century, to validate the person of the king as God's appointment. Political reality is more complex. The direct hereditary succession was not established until well after the Reformation. The archbishop anoints the sovereign, who sits under a canopy, from the Ampulla, which is the shape of an eagle and the oil is poured into a spoon. The monarch is marked on the hands, breast and head, with the sign of the cross.

Shakespeare puts these words into the mouth of Henry V:

No thou proud dream,
That play'st so subtly with a king's repose;
I am a king that find thee, and I know
'Tis not the balm, the sceptre and the ball.
The sword, the mace, the crown imperial,
The intertissued robe of gold and pearl,
Not, not all these, thrice-gorgeous ceremony,
Not all these laid in bed majestical,
Can sleep so soundly as the wretched slave. (Act IV, 2, 275ff)

and Richard II defends his kingship:

Not all the water in the rough rude sea
Can wash the balm off from an anointed king;
The breath of worldly men cannot depose in
The deputy elected by the Lord. (Act III, 2, 54-7)

But Bolingbroke could and did, and Richard is murdered and Henry IV duly anointed and crowned.

After the anointing the King is dressed in semi-priestly robes: a full, sleeveless garment which is the robe of purity and equivalent to the alb. Then a super-tunica embroidered with flowers and lined in scarlet, and this has the stole royal and a robe of cloth of gold over it: the monarch has in the midst of this dressing received the spurs and a sword, symbols of chivalry. Then seated in the coronation chair the orb is given and the ring. The orb is God's rule over temporal authority and the ring, as with bishops, about marriage to the land: there are also the sceptre and rod which represent kingly power and equity and mercy. Then comes the moment of crowning. St Edward's Crown was made for the coronation of Charles II, after the regalia had largely been destroyed during the Commonwealth. The title is of course significant. Following the coronation homage is made, first by the archbishop and then by the senior peer of each rank. The Eucharist then continues.

It seems to me extraordinary that this ceremony was accepted with little question in 1952 but would not be carried out in the same way today. Except that the Moderator of the Church of Scotland presented the Bible, it was a wholly Anglican service. No role for other church leaders let alone people of other faiths.

The rite has a mythical quality because it makes of one person, now simply by accident of birth, a semi-sacerdotal figure. Despite the rebellions and revolutions, the kings killed in battle, murdered in dungeons and even executed on the scaffold, the English on the whole believed the myth of their sovereigns. It is still there in the way that we look back at kings without really taking on board their actual characters. Henry VIII's arrogance, capricious cruelty and cynical use of power, his over-weening self-importance are overlooked because he was king.

Statues of kings are to be found in or on most greater churches. James I and Charles I stand at the west end of Winchester. Ripon, York, Canterbury have rows of them on the pulpitum. Lincoln has a frieze of them over the west doors. Chichester has paintings of them. They appear too in windows and as corbel stones.

Kings are buried too with ornate tombs as befits the head of state, many in Westminster Abbey but others elsewhere; William II perhaps in Winchester. There is some doubt about this, although he died in an accident, or perhaps murdered, in the nearby New Forest. John is in Worcester, Edward II, also murdered, in Gloucester. He was a potential saint, which would have done Gloucester's reputation and coffers a great deal of good but the process never got very far. Henry IV and the Black Prince are buried in Canterbury and two queens were given burial in Peterborough: Katherine of Aragon and Mary, Queen of Scots; the former dying in a kind of disgrace, and the other executed by Elizabeth I. James I moved his mother's remains to Westminster, but the Spanish queen still lies in Peterborough. Her first husband, Prince Arthur, who died very young, lies in a chantry chapel at Worcester. How history would have been different had Arthur not died and therefore Henry VIII probably not have been king.

The monarchy continues but power, government, is actually in the hands of politicians and has been for several centuries. The reality of government no longer fits the myth. The Queen remains the symbol of statehood and government but does it make sense for a completely secular government to be symbolized with such a religious myth, and one in which few people believe anyway? But the coronation rite explains the presence of monarchs in the greater churches. Up to the Reformation it is about the religious nature of the monarchy and it also points up the fact that the ceremony is performed by the Archbishop of Canterbury. And indeed those archbishops had helped to forge the English nation into a single realm. Kings were not allowed to forget that there had been archbishops longer than there had been kings.

The shift of power at the Reformation was considerable, for Henry didn't so much abolish papal power as assume it himself. The 'Supreme Governor' title, although now exercised through Synod and Parliament, was all too real a power in the sixteenth and seventeenth centuries.

The Church does however support the state. Both Peter and Paul in the New Testament commend prayer for the sovereign, and theirs were pagan emperors. The prayer in the BCP Eucharist which speaks of us 'knowing whose authority she hath' goes too far, I guess. Do we believe that the Queen has God's authority?

Parliament has met in a number of other places than Westminster. In the nearby Chapter House of the Abbey, and in Shrewsbury and Lincoln. The Barons met in Bury St Edmunds' Abbey to discuss their plans for imposing what became known as Magna Carta on King John. Their coats of arms adorn the quire of the Cathedral there, rightly, as men who were inspired by justice for all and sought to limit the unfettered powers of kings.

One annual ceremony once always held in Westminster but now touring the greater churches is the Royal Maundy. It is the symbol of humility recalling Jesus' washing of the disciples' feet at the Last Supper (John 13.3-17). Medieval kings actually washed feet, but the Queen gives purses of specially minted coins to men and women in recognition of their Christian service. Maundy is a corruption from *mandatum*, the Latin for command. Jesus said, A new commandment I give to you, that you love another. The Queen reigns as a Christian monarch and despite all the controversies of the last decade she continues to do her duty and that, with not only her evident good humour, but I suspect also with affection and even love. Seated in the House of Lords, wearing the robes and the crown, reading the Queen's Speech, which we all know is actually the government's, we see a person of strength and courage, but also of lowliness. That combination of royal splendour but reading someone else's words seems to me to express that element of service which is at the heart of Christian truth.

The Crown still exercises patronage in the Church, but as with all other matters this is exercised almost entirely through politicians.

When we are visiting churches and see the tombs and statues of kings perhaps we should give some thought to the relationship between the Church and the state: how do we see government? Is sovereignty God's which He delegates as it were to us, or is it ours to exercise through the democratic process?

And what of the future? Do we want our head of state to be a semi-priestly figure and how do we incorporate into a ceremony to inaugurate a reign the fact that we are a multi-cultural society with many people of other faiths and of none? The Queen looks set long to reign over us, but the issues need thinking about now.

CHAPTER XVII

Episcopal

W e move from monarch to bishop and to the exercise of authority in the Church. The monarch's role is now symbolic but perhaps because of the involvement of lay people in the Church's structures bishops have become more powerful. The creation of first the Church Assembly and then the General Synod has given the House of Bishops a new authority as we have tried to marry a degree of democracy with being an episcopal Church. *The* pattern of authority must be Jesus. He said that he was among us as one who serves. This service of leadership so easily shades off into the mere exercise of power and lording it over others. The thrones and tombs of medieval bishops certainly tend more to power and worldly glory than to service, although there is a distinction to be made between the man himself and the trappings of office. The titles, for example, of degrees of reverence from plain Reverend to Most, for an archbishop, are about the office rather than the person. But should those who hold office in the Church need to require these things? The saints speaks to us through the way they lived. not from the style of clothes, or the titles with which they are addressed. It takes a genuine humility for someone to fill an important office with true service – and the issue cannot be fudged. Somehow the person's inner attitudes become all too apparent.

The Church by its nature is episcopal – at least those parts of the Church which build and continue to build and use these greater churches.

Writing in the 1930s Gabriel Hebert was scathing about Anglican bishops.[1] The office was misunderstood, he said, because it was regarded simply as a convenient method of organization but that misses the real meaning, and that is lost when the Divine character of the Church is lost. Hebert draws out three aspects of episcopal order. First, unity: the bishop represents catholicity and the unity of all Christian people. Secondly, he links the local church (local is always diocesan) with every other local church and he takes his people with him into the councils of the Church. And thirdly, he links this generation with past and future: he is consecrated into the same office as the bishops of the past, and of the future.

Ministry is Christ's and is given to the whole Church but is focussed in the bishops. This is one of God's great gifts to the Church: the service which the Church receives from its own ministers. It is not about management but humble service. The ARCIC documents have given us a greater understanding of the bishop's role.

> Pastoral authority belongs primarily to the bishop, who is responsible for preserving and promoting the integrity of the koinonia in order to further the Church's response to the Lordship of Christ and its commitment to mission. Koinonia is realised not only in local Christian communities, but also in the communion of these communities with one another... The Bishop expresses this unity of his church with the others. This is symbolised by the participation of several bishops in his ordination.[2]

There is also the question of archbishops, primates. Again ARCIC: primacy is 'not an autocratic power over the Church but a service in and to the Church which is a communion in faith and charity of local Churches'. St Gregory assumed when he sent Augustine to England in 597 that the old pattern of civil government still existed here. His information was distinctly out of date. He planned two provinces centred on London and York, but as we all know Augustine's see was Canterbury and it was under later men that York became archiepiscopal. There have been great rows down the medieval centuries over precedence, hardly what one ought to expect from Christian leadership. The compromise, which places York most definitely second, is in their primatial titles: York is Primate of England, and Canterbury of All England. That frankly is ridiculous. Until 1914 the dioceses in Wales were part of the province of Canterbury, but now the Welsh bishops elect one of themselves to be Archbishop.

The things we can see in the greater churches are episcopal chairs and tombs, and elsewhere palaces and chapter houses speak to us of authority. The Greek word for chair is *kathedra*, hence our word cathedral. It is a seat of authority and of teaching. Remarkably few of the present thrones date from before the nineteenth century. In Norwich fragments of the present throne date from c630. It was restored to its original position in the present cathedral in 1959. This is within the apse of the Presbytery, behind the high altar. The chair is at the head of a flight of stairs and beneath it is a kind of chimney. This connects the throne with a reliquary which was housed below in the ambulatory, as if the power of the relics is being conducted to the present bishop.

Tatton-Brown[3] believes the frithstool at Hexham to be an early episcopal chair. That is certainly of Saxon date. In Canterbury the Purbeck stone chair of St Augustine is of the thirteenth century. From about 1800 until 1977 it stood in the Corona but was replaced in its earlier position above the high altar in 1977. During the nineteenth and twentieth centuries it had been brought to the pulpitum steps for the enthronement of archbishops.

Bishop Hatfield of Durham had constructed a gallery above his future tomb in the cathedral where the throne is set. It is high above the floor of the cathedral against the south arcade. The balustrade is later. It bears the arms of Bishop Crewe (1674-1721). In Hereford the bishop's chair is part of the early fourteenth century choir stalls and similarly the Bishop of Ely has a stall in the fourteenth century ones there. He was abbot so has the southern return stall, normally occupied by deans in other cathedrals. So of the 14 cathedrals which existed before 1066 and the 2 creations of the twelfth century (Ely 1109 and Carlisle 1133) and the 6 of the sixteenth century, only 6 have medieval chairs. These are all simple pieces of furniture but then you may recall the simplicity of the Coronation Chair made in 1300 by Master Walter of Durham to contain the Stone of Scone, now, alas, removed.

However, the cathedrals have many tombs of abbots and bishops and these become increasingly ornate as the centuries pass: they begin with simple ledger stones usually inscribed and with abbatial or epsicopal figures. These gave way to low relief carvings and which themselves later became transformed into effigies. As the figures became more ornate, and usually richly painted, so the surroundings became richer too, with ornate canopies. The finest of these are often the chantries of the sixteenth century. After the reformation episcopal tombs followed the pattern of secular ones: but with standing figures, reclining ones, even kneeling ones, they were rarely sober.

Then with the return of all things medieval in the nineteenth century, came once more the recumbent effigies, canopies, angels, coats of arms and all kinds of ornamentation. Christopher Wordsworth's in Lincoln and Samuel Wilberforce's in Oxford are typical. Usually these were no longer actually tombs, but memorials. However, they speak as with a megaphone about how episcopacy was seen in the nineteenth century. Such tombs continued though: there is one in splendid green bronze in the ruins at Coventry but more modest plaques are now placed to recall our bishops to mind. (I like John Robinson's gravestone in North Yorkshire. It is a simple moorland boulder with his name and dates and with a small mitre as the only thing to say who he was.)

Some modern bishops still sit in rather prelatical thrones: Sir Charles Nicholson designed a number in the 1930s which have canopies and spires, Leicester and Sheffield among them.

Medieval bishops were feudal lords, great landowners and frequently in the royal service. In an age when travel was difficult and dangerous they travelled a great deal and this accounts for their numerous palaces and castles. The Bishops of Winchester had one in the city and a kind of summer retreat at Bishop's Waltham, a few miles south; in addition, Farnham Castle and a palace in Southwark. The diocese of Lincoln sported palaces in the city – (its ruins next to a nineteenth-century house built for Bishop King are on the slope below the cathedral) at Nettleham, north-east of Lincoln, Stow Park (Lincs), Fingest (Bucks), Lyddington (Leics), Louth (Lincs) and Buckden (Hunts), together with castles at Newark, Sleaford and Banbury. But if the bishop and his household were to visit the diocese in any practical way, at least most of these houses were necessary. Modern bishops with such large dioceses would use helicopters and sleep in the same bed each night, but medieval bishops had perforce to have beds all over the place.

Chapter houses we have already discussed. They were places of debate and decision, but their design reveals much about how this was done. In some the seats of dean and archdeacons have some distinction from the rest, although this is usually modest, but basically these rooms are circular or octagonal, and the masons eventually found ways of doing away with the central piers. Around the walls run stone seats and these have small canopies or more often blind arcading.

These are places for open discussion where everyone has a voice. I wonder how often that was true in practice but it was Benedict's intention. He says in the Rule that the abbot is to consult even the youngest members of the community and implies that they have more wisdom than their elders. That remains a radical idea. We tend to assume that you have to serve years before being allowed to make a contribution, and despite our youth-driven culture, young people are not assumed to have even as much, let alone more, wisdom than their elders.

All this makes us think about leadership, authority, decision making both in the Christian community and in all other areas of life. The tombs speak to us of power and wealth, the episcopal seats on the whole are not immodest and provide settings for the Christian leader who needs to be seen to preside. Very few thrones are so placed that the bishop presides from them visibly: Portsmouth, Norwich, Canterbury are among the few. Chapter houses speak of open debate and decision making. But how do we exercise and receive authority?

The Rule of St Benedict has much to offer in our collection of evidence. A great deal in Benedict's writing is about the abbot but I think what he says can apply to anyone in a position of authority, whether in the Church or in industry or education. First, he reminds us firmly that the abbot represents Christ. To stand in the place of Christ is a heavy role but are we not all called to be Christ-like? And if we who are under authority can see Christ in those over us it makes our working with and for them much easier. It is about having trust and respect for those in authority. Our age is corrosive of authority and impoverishes our common life in that way. Authority is a great gift to maintain order and purpose, to create unity, but the authority must be exercised with humility. How important it is that the right people are appointed, and so Benedict writes at length about the kind of men abbots should be. They are shepherds bearing the blame for any lack of profit in the sheep (2.7) Responsibility is important in leaders. The buck may not finally stop here, but they do have responsibilities. 'The abbot is to indicate what is good and holy more by example than by word' (12). Well, we all know that what we do speaks a lot louder than what we say. 'He ought not to love one more than another.' Fairness, equity are vital in leadership but that doesn't mean treating all the same. 'He must be flexible treating each one according to his character and understanding.' The abbot is to be a worthy steward, always to set mercy above judgement, to hate evil but love the brethren. To aim at being loved rather than feared.

'Because the abbot is believed to hold the place of Christ, he should be called Lord and abbot, not out of presumption on his part but out of reverence and love for Christ' (63.13). He quotes St Paul in the Letter to the Romans: Out do one another in showing honour (Rom 12.10).

This also raises the question of obedience again. As we have seen it is about listening and responding positively. Benedict says, 'no one should presume to contend defiantly with his abbot' (3.9) because the authority is Christ's and in obeying the monks are obeying Christ. Obedience should be with 'joy and good grace, for with bad grace and grumbling, even in his heart, he will not find acceptance with God' (5.17).

ARCIC reminds us of the the need for a focus of leadership and unity in the authority of the bishop, and within the parish context, of the priest: the goal of ordained ministry is to serve. The New Testament is full of images: servant of Christ as well as of the Church; herald, ambassador, teacher, shepherd, steward; these are all about service offered in love and humility because they all partake of the ministry of Christ which is marked by humble, loving service. For many of us we do not see authority, leadership as a gift to us, but it is. It enables us, when exercised well, to fulfil our own role effectively.

Abbots were to seek counsel, even from the junior members of the community and then make decisions that all will obey. That is one model of leadership.

The abbots of the regular canons had something of this about them, and the fact that they used this title is significant, but perhaps they tended toward the leadership model of deans. Deans are certainly the leaders of their chapters but decisions are made by consensus, or at least by majority. Deans do not act alone, as an abbot does. It is always the dean and chapter. This lack of power can create difficulties but there are strong arguments for this kind of balanced leadership: one that seeks common ground and brings everyone on board rather than being autocratic and dictatorial which is the danger of the abbatial authority if it is not exercised as Christ's and received in the same way. There are questions here about how we exercise and receive authority in the workplace and in society generally.

One is led to think about PCCs and the family too. Authority within the family is a touchy issue, involving issues of gender and a modern desire not to acknowledge the need for authority. Very few brides choose to promise to obey their husbands and increasingly the men do not want to be obeyed, but the issues of how decisions are to be made need to be tackled seriously.

Often priests overawe their PCCs, but really they are like deans. Decisions are actually vicar and PCC together. But a problem arises over the fact that he is ordained and therefore carries a different weight of authority, which it has to be said has been used unjustly by some clergy and the laity have too long allowed them to get away with it. There are, I believe, inherent problems in being both a spiritual leader and one who has to deal with other issues in an authoritative way. I do not say authoritarian: there is no room for that in the Christian Church. But often hard decisions, needful for the fruitful life of the parish, are not taken because of the pastoral implications. Would it not be better to have two centres of authority: one spiritual, the other managerial?

Benedict quotes Ecclesiasticus (32.19): 'Do all things with counsel and afterwards you will not regret it.' That seems to me excellent advice, as do some words of St Gregory: 'See everything, ignore much, correct little.' Authority needs to be exercised with a light touch.

Finally a word on chapter houses that seems to fit better here than anywhere else. They are not all circular: rectangular ones are at Bristol and Oxford, Canterbury, Durham and Gloucester but these tend to be earlier in date. Bristol's is a superb piece of Norman architecture. Worcester is early twelfth century and was originally circular but in the fourteenth century was redesigned as a decagon. That and those at Lincoln, Lichfield, Westminster, Wells and Salisbury are all of the thirteenth century and have central piers. York and Southwell are c1290 and are without that central support. On the whole these buildings were simply functional and therefore remain unaltered. Many of them are really exciting spaces. With the tiny chapters of today they are rarely used for chapter meetings but provide space for school assemblies, lectures, exhibitions, and even parties. These simple buildings speak directly to us of how decisions ought to be made. There is an essential equality about the seating arrangements. That process of listening and of responding positively, which is how I think obedience actually works, can be seen in the architecture.

The cathedrals of England are now in the midst of an important change in their system of governance. The desire for change comes out of the modern obsession with accountability. No-one could accuse Benedict of not wanting his abbots to be accountable, but it was to God not to others. Cathedrals are places with a distinct role in our society although the number of books and articles, written often by people serving in them, seem to raise many questions about the role. I would have thought there was no doubt for there is an enormous reservoir of support for our greater churches. The flourishing Friends organizations are proof of that to say nothing of the thousands of visitors. Cathedrals are very much on the frontline of the Church's mission.

Under the new arrangements each cathedral is to have a Cathedral Council which will have representatives of the wider community as well as of regular worshippers and the Diocese. Its role is to provide general oversight of the cathedral's life and it will be chaired by a distinguished member of the community. The Bishop, strangely, cannot be the chairman because he is Visitor, but will have an ex officio place on the Council. What does that say about our beliefs about bishops? The Dean and Chapter are also members. The Council is not an administrative body: that function is to be exercised by an Administrative Chapter which is the present chapter with additions. There will be between two and seven others, of whom at least two-thirds must be lay, and for a period of three years. The idea is to bring in people with administrative and management skills. The present Greater Chapter gets a new name: the College of Canons. Their function remains much as it is at present, as a forum to be consulted as appropriate.

As part of the new process the statutes of cathedrals will be revised. I am wary of 'management' but the greater churches have large budgets and they need to be run efficiently and well, but it is vital that those who can influence and decide the issues that face them should do so from within the Christian faith. That doesn't mean they must be clergy, but we must not find the managers' policies being those which are followed. The Church is not a plc. It does not have the character of a business although it has income, expenditure, and runs a number of business enterprises. We have to find ways of maintaining these great buildings as places of living prayer and worship. The pressures are great. For not only do the regulations about church buildings continue to increase, there are the strings attached to the acceptance of grants from the government (through whatever agency) and the costs of repair and conservation mount. All the time there is pressure from the amenity agencies: English Heritage, the Victorian Society, and increasingly people generally are not willing to allow the Church to run its own institutions, not because we are not reasonably good at it, but because in our desire to maintain our churches as churches we might not protect the heritage and the non-worshippers' right of access. It is a tightrope, but we must hope that the new ways of governing cathedrals and the new statutes will manage to get the balance right.

The rhythms and balance of the Benedictine way are reflected in the architecture they built. This is Peterborough.

The mightiest example of Benedictine architecture is this nave, with some of the earliest vaulting, at Durham.

The crypt at Worcester Cathedral – a forest of stumpy pillars creating wonderful inter-connected spaces. It dates from 1084.

The crypt capitals at Canterbury are richly carved.

The Cistercian monasteries soon fell into ruin after they were dissolved by Henry VIII. This is the presbytery at Rievaulx.

Uniquely, Lichfield Cathedral has three spires, but the whole exterior has been much restored. The red sandstone of which it is built is quickly eroded.

One of the finest Gothic churches anywhere, this is a view of York Minster from the south-east.

Malmesbury was rebuilt from 1180: the arcade and the gallery survive, but the clerestory and vaulting date from the fourteenth century. This kind of alteration was quite common. Many greater churches had new vaults built. Other examples are at Christchurch and Tewskesbury.

Another new vault is this one at Oxford. It is a fan-vault with pendants and really spectacular.

The Presbytery of Norwich Cathedral where the Romanesque architecture was transformed in the fifteenth century, making it higher and much lighter. The vault has a great many bosses.

Crowland, once a greater church, is now a parish church using just part of the north aisle. The west facade and important sculpture give us a hint of its former splendour.

CHAPTER XVIII

Pre-1066 and Romanesque

In the early years after the Normans' victory of October 1066 there was an explosion of new building work all over England. Castles, of course, but also monasteries, cathedrals and parish churches. There were fifteen major churches under construction before 1100 and another five by 1150. Many of these buildings were going up on the sites of older buildings. Canterbury was the scene of new work in 1070 but the older buildings there dated from the turn of the seventh century. St Etheldreda's monastery at Ely had been founded in 670. The Norman abbot began his rebuilding on the same site in about 1083. Occasionally it was an entirely new site, or at least a new site for a greater church. Norwich, for example, was begun in 1096, but there had been other buildings on the site, including some parish churches.

However, in a number of places there is physical evidence of earlier buildings. At Westminster an expert eye can discern passageways that remain from the Confessor's monastery only completed at the end of 1065. St Wilfred had founded churches at Hexham and Ripon and in both cases the crypts survive beneath much later churches. These date from c670. That at Hexham was only rediscovered in 1726 and some of its stone had been taken from the Roman fort at Corbridge. Similarly old materials were used in the construction of St Albans: notably the red Roman tiles of the central tower, but there are reused Saxon materials; the colonettes of the triforium in the transepts, for example.

A number of other pieces of sculpture survive: the fragments of the bishop's throne at Norwich from the late seventh century; a cross shaft of similar date at Ely. From c800 the Hedda stone at Peterborough and a font at Wells. A roundel of Christ at Gloucester is of the mid-tenth century and a Harrowing of Hell at Bristol is of c1050. The frithstool at Hexham as we have seen might be the original Anglo-Saxon throne. There is also evidence that the surviving west front at Sherborne was the east wall of a large Anglo-Saxon tower with north and south transepts.

Archaeology has also revealed earlier buildings at Winchester, Exeter, Wells, Peterborough and Canterbury.[1]

Stand at the west end of Ely or Peterborough, Durham or Gloucester and you are looking down the long nave of a Romanesque church. The eastern ones seem especially long, rather narrow and have wooden ceilings: Peterborough's is original, Ely's painted in the nineteenth century. The length is divided into bays and every bay is identical. You only had to design one and then build as many as you wanted. This is much like the Benedictine day. There is a regular rhythm of day and night, and the round of services from prayers in the night, through the hours of the day to Compline as the monks prepared for sleep: their day moved from choir to refectory, back to choir, to cloister, to choir again, to dormitory; a consistent pattern day after day. It is a quiet, contented rhythm into which the individual finds his place. It is a community rhythm. How much we need those fixed points, those repeated patterns of living. It is one of those aspects of stability, so important a part of the Benedictine rule. We need roots, we need pattern, we need structure. This architecture can teach us to value the repetition. No two days are actually alike, for all sorts of circumstances are constantly changing, but those changes make more sense when set against a regular background. I think the monks moving against their strict, architectural setting is a good image of that. From the regularity of our lives can come the rubato (that stretching of the value of beats in music) and the syncopation, when the accent is suddenly placed off the beat. Rubato and syncopation only have any sense at all when set against the regular rhythms. The freedom of a holiday is only real when it stands against the normal pattern of work. Modern times tend to regard the routine as dull and it can be. We need to recognize that living has its dull routine and come to terms with it. Fortunately most of us do, for if life is to be good, to grow and develop we need regular food, exercise, sleep, work, leisure, prayer. The peace and strength of these Norman naves remind us of all this.

The bays are regular but the aisles, with their lower groined or ribbed vaults, and the much higher central space are designed for movement, especially processions. There is too much of the vertical in the architecture to make for rapid movement forward: for the arches of arcade, gallery and clerestory sit straight upon each other, but between them the horizontal string courses lead us forward, but with slow step. The three levels have different designs, and at Peterborough there are interesting details. The tympana of the gallery (the area above the arches) for example, and there are mouldings and decorations like the dog-tooth and sometimes zig-zag. But this style draws us into contemplation. Benedictines for all their activities are essentially contemplatives: a great many hours are spent in the quire singing offices or involved in private reading and study. The relative austerity of this style underlines this inner life. The strength, solidity, mass, the sombre tone makes for an ordered, firm spirituality, something deeply rooted, that takes the ordinary, the mundane and finds God in that.

These naves are places of refuge. The sheer quantity of stone, in areas of plain surface, or in the multi-form piers, provides an enclosure which parallels the experience of God's love enclosing us with protection. The dominant virtue is faith – seeing value and purpose in the regular order of daily life. The Benedictine community is a family doing ordinary things in an extraordinary way, said Thomas Merton.

We can find God in the ordinary – even in the apparently boring. You have to stick with things to find out. Those seeking quick returns will not find them with Benedictine or with Romanesque architecture.

There are, however, moments of drama as well as grandeur. The sculptures are often dynamic and exciting. I think of the Prior's Door at Ely and the crypt capitals at Canterbury, or the west facade at Rochester. The prior entering the nave at Ely was reminded daily of Christ and of his needing to be Christ-like, for as the head of his community (the bishop was the abbot, but not part of the day-to-day life of the monastery) the others would regard him as Christ. At Canterbury the figures are from the realms of fable and are executed with a wild imagination but with technical mastery: weird, amusing, puzzling; musical goats, two-headed monsters, full of spirit. They may have significant meanings but if so they are lost to us. At Lincoln too there are sculptures telling mainly biblical tales with vivid detail.

Exterior decoration – circles, lozenges, blind arcades, quatrefoils, slit windows, various mouldings – were sometimes used to great effect, again notably at Norwich. Try to see the tower without the much later spire. The unique design of Ely's west tower and transept, alas lopsided because the northern half collapsed, and with a much later porch, is a rich example. Perhaps more typical exteriors are at Southwell and Tewskesbury.

The West Country naves – Gloucester, Hereford, and Tewskesbury – have huge cylinder piers. These give an extra sense of stillness, but also of subtle movement, as one's eye moves around the surface of the columns in a kind of undulating pattern. The abrupt change from circular pier to moulded arch is also a point of stasis: a slowing down, a difficult junction. We have need of those things too: to linger, to take time, to reflect. The monk's day is busy, moving from activity to activity, but the movement is balanced as the bays are and a great deal of day and night is spent in the almost still rhythms of plainsong: space and time in the flow for being with God. Can we who live our life in the world, with homes, families and other commitments find ways of living which include times of stillness, times of being with God? If we are to find a real balance, and a wholeness, it is vital that we do. We have come to see monasticism as an extraordinary way of life but Benedict was creating a very ordinary institution: a family living, praying, working, relaxing together in which each individual could grow fully into himself and thus find holiness.

Durham brings together the multiform piers of eastern England and the circular piers of the West and combines them in a rich, duple bay system and crowns it all with a ribbed vault. The massive piers with their rich decoration have a wild exuberance. The pattern of the arches in the ribs of the vaulting, slightly pointed transverse arches rising above the multiform piers, and the crossed arches rising from the same point and from above the circular ones are a delight to the eye. The horizontal features are few and the sense of movement forward comes from the vaulting. This place speaks to us of a God of power, of solemnity, of protection and grace.

We are reminded that the builders were Norman in the century or so after William's victory at Hastings. They were meant to impress, to overawe and subdue. Nine hundred years later they still have that feel. Is this the God who is the Father of Our Lord Jesus Christ? Hasn't Benedict's father to a family become a powerful feudal lord? Aren't these buildings also instruments of oppression? As the medieval centuries passed the actual life of Benedictine communities brought an immense richness to the communities around. They were schools, hospitals, guesthouses, places of learning and beauty, places in which in a diversity of ways the Gospel was lived out. They produced administrators, scholars, craftsmen, writers, men of prayer and untold numbers of holy lives.

The Benedictines altered their buildings by adding towers, inserting new windows, raising vaults and sometimes tried to remodel whole sections of the church, but apart from accidents of fire and earthquake, and collapses due to poor foundations, they rarely simply rebuilt. The cathedral priory of Canterbury is the exception, but then Canterbury was not just any Benedictine house. This bringing up to date by mere alteration of windows, roofs and so on speaks to me of the value that the past has for us. But it also shows that the style suited their living: the massive, simple style drew those who lived around these churches into the deep rhythms of life. Life lived at a pace which enables deep thought and prayer and which brings peace and contentment through its stability and ordinariness.

These are virtues we can bring to our living now: rhythms, a slower pace, a regular balance of activities – work, leisure, sleep – a moderation, a humane quality. A willingness to find delight and joy and peace in the given: not running after the novel, but sticking with the well-known, well-used paths and in this commitment discovering growth and nourishment.

Benedictinism is a way of living, not an order like the Franciscans or Jesuits, so each abbey was its own family – the Rule has always been adapted to local circumstances and the architecture is treated in the same way.

We don't see these churches exactly as they were built. They are nearly always lighter because of windows inserted into the gallery and often nave windows are altered too. It is interesting to stand in the cloister at Norwich and observe all the different layers, like some multi-layered sandwich, and to work out what was there originally and what are the changes.

But the other change is the lack of colour. Most of these buildings would have had paintwork everywhere. So the austere stone-coloured churches were once brilliant. Can you imagine those designs in Durham filled with bright blues, reds and greens?

Not all the early Romanesque churches are Benedictine. Of those begun before 1100 Lincoln and Chichester were not. Very little of the Norman cathedral at Lincoln survives except embedded in the west front. At Chichester a fire in the early twelfth century meant that changes were possible and my feeling is that the changes made would probably not have been made by a Benedictine house. Initially they remodelled the arcades with Purbeck shafts, and by rebuilding the clerestory. Later they remodelled the retroquire and in the thirteenth century threw out the nave walls to make more chapels and gave the building a vault. Despite all these changes I think the building retains a strong sense of the Romanesque.

Other cathedrals have Norman elements – the transeptal towers at Exeter, for example – but it is always interesting as we visit greater churches to look for Romanesque parts, so I leave you to find them.

CHAPTER XIX

Cistercians – from Romanesque to Gothic

To look carefully at the nave of Selby Abbey is to observe a gradual shift from Romanesque to Gothic: the shape of the arches changes from round to pointed, and we can see this as the work developed from bay to bay and even from side to side. The Galilee Chapel at Durham has tall thin piers quite different from those in the nave but is clearly not Gothic. However, the retroquire at Chichester, the rebuilding at Canterbury in the 1170s and the naves of Wells and Llandaff are definitely Gothic. And when you come to look at the Cistercian churches of the early to mid-twelfth century you feel these are a kind of transition between the two styles. Indeed what the textbooks call 'transitional'. Otto Von Simson argues that far from being a development Gothic is the antithesis of Romanesque. He's writing about French architecture and when we look at Abbot Suger's rebuilding of St Denis, near Paris in the Ile de France we can see his point. 'Gothic', he writes, 'is not the heir but the rival of Romanesque, created as its emphatic antithesis.'[1] My own feeling is that that may be true in France, but that in England Gothic didn't come suddenly in the one building but was rather a process of becoming.

Before we go on to explore the spirituality of Gothic we must make a visit to a Cistercian Church which, except for two where the gatehouse chapel became the parish church (Hailes in Glos and Kirkstead in Lincs), we cannot do because all the Cistercian churches lie in ruins: Fountains, Rievaulx, Kirkstall, Meaux, Sawley and many others. Their remote sites meant that apart from quarries they were of almost no use once the monks had been evicted. I want to take you to Kirkstall in Leeds but before that something about the Cistercians themselves.

There was a simplicity, an austerity about these churches despite their size and grandeur. Zarnecki comments that the only dull Romanesque capitals are in Cistercian buildings,[2] but then he is the expert on Romanesque carving and all early medieval sculpture. Cistercian churches had none of the decoration of Ely or Durham or of the early Gothic churches like Wells or Canterbury. The monks chose sites in wild and remote country. Cîteaux itself was typical. They were societies separated from the wider society, self-contained, self-reliant. They were linked into an Order but loosely compared with the Cluniac houses or the later friars. They were free, having no links with the Crown, had no tenants, novices came at the earliest at sixteen, there were no boys, no schools and apart from Orders and Holy Oils they were independent of the bishops too.

They returned to the letter of St Benedict's Rule: the rhythm of liturgical prayer, private reading and manual work. The liturgy was pruned from the excesses that Cluny had demanded, so that, for example, there was only one Mass for the community except on a few feast days. Their diet was confined to bread, vegetables, fish, flour, eggs, milk and cheese: and all of that they produced for themselves or went without. The lands they owned required a lot of work so they developed two kinds of brothers: the choir brothers who sang the opus Dei as the Rule requires and the *conversi* whose main task was manual work and who used a simpler liturgy in the nave. Often they were small communities, perhaps starting with twenty-four brothers divided between choir monks and *conversi*. The order spread rapidly across Europe.

The churches typifying this reformed monastic life were of surpassing beauty, says Dom David Knowles, but that beauty was not sought.[3] There was no ornament or superfluity in the liturgical life: crucifixes of wood, candelabra of iron, chasubles of fustian, albs of linen, chalices of silver rather than gold. They had renounced the feudal sources of wealth.

The order was devoted to Our Lady and their white robes were adopted in honour of her. All their churches are dedicated in her honour. Their simple, hard lifestyle was lived with the three-fold vows of St Benedict's Rule: stability, conversion of life, and obedience, with Our Lady as a model of perfection. There was an enormous contrast with the Benedictines. The argument between them we find personified in Suger and St Bernard of Clairvaux: the one using vast resources, intellectual and economic, to build a magnificent, richly decorated abbey, and the other using his intellectual powers at full stretch to condemn luxury and indolence.

But let us go to Kirkstall. The ruins are set in an open park very close to the A68 in the western suburbs of Leeds. Most are surrounded by iron railings so you have to peer through and crane your neck to see. This is a pity because the walls stand to roof height and this enables anyone to imagine the complete buildings fairly easily.

The nave has eight bays; the piers on square bases constructed of eight shafts, alternately major and minor. The aisles are narrow but based on the square of the bay, just as the nave width is two bays. The arcade arches are just pointed but the clerestory windows are round-headed. The west facade has a doorway under a gable with two round-headed windows above. The turrets here and elsewhere, and the gable window are later additions. All this is severely plain. The transepts have aisles on the eastern side divided into three chapels with pointed barrel vaults. The central tower was originally very low, just above the roofs around it. The present ruined traceries are a later heightening. The presbytery is unaisled, square ended and only two bays. To the south you can walk around the cloister and visit the Chapter House which was built in two stages: first, the vestibule which has a central pier of eight shafts, and in the room itself some of the shafts are keeled: that is to say that the shape of the shaft comes to a sharp point. Typically the refectory is built north/south on the south side of the cloister. This pattern is basic to all Cistercian houses: simple, detached, pure, austere and originally remote. That remoteness and isolation is more obvious at Roche, a few miles from Maltby. Arriving there you hear the sounds of sheep, of running water and birdsong, unchanged down the centuries. The church which reminds me most of these Cistercian ones but is still in use is Hexham Abbey. That was built for Augustinian canons in the 1180s but has this mixture of round and pointed arches, and the quire piers are much like those at Byland Abbey, with major and minor shafts which are keeled.

The word which sums up this spirituality is humility, which is seen so clearly in the life of Our Lady, St Mary. Humility is about seeing things as they truly are. It is about a recognition of ourselves, sinners that we are, and yet loved by God. As the word itself suggests humility is about being earthed. In Our Lady we see that lowliness of spirit which is direct and open to God. We see her total obedience borne of her simplicity and made warm by her love. If we are to be humble we must learn to put others first. We must learn to listen to God and to respond without hesitation to His bidding, and to obey with joy. Another feature of Cistercian life was an emphasis on friendship which finds its classic expression in the life of St Aelred of Rievaulx, who wrote about spiritual friendship and practised it in his community. That must have been doubly hard for him in an all-male environment because of his homosexuality.

Friendship is much underrated in our society. The lack of true friends places an overemphasis on our marriage partners. We put too great a weight on the one relationship which often cracks under the strain. People are wary of friendships especially with persons of the same sex, for our world tends to assume that all close relationships must be sexual – and they most certainly are not. St Aelred's writings can help us to see the importance of intimate friendships, and did not Jesus call his disciples friend?

These ruins are still extraordinarily evocative of Cistercian spirituality. Even from the fragments we can see their simplicity and imagine the austere, humble life of the monks. They draw us away from the world into an internal awareness of God. These places were built so that Christ's light, light seen in the clear light that flooded these buildings, might allow men to withdraw and find their lives offered to God in union with the sacrifice of Christ. This is not a harsh austerity but one filled with joy. The Anglican Cistercian monastery at Ewell writes of its own life:

> Every day the monk tries to love Jesus Christ more. He who first loved us unto death. The monk's life is an offering of love, from the heart, in union with the sacrifice of Christ. In the seclusion of the monastery, separated from all, the monk together with his brothers seeks to work with the risen Lord Jesus Christ for the salvation of all his fellow men. He does this humbly: and in constant prayer and penitence he is closely joined to all. His life is a pilgrimage in which he draws other men and women with him to God our Father, the source of all our love and hope. In his heart there is joy and peace, despite the difficulties, for he knows that in faithfulness and perseverance to the end all shall be well and all manner of thing shall be well – with God.[4]

This is a vocation for very few, but we can all learn from it. Learn about humility, about simplicity of life, about giving our lives to God, in whatever way and place He calls us.

CHAPTER XX

Gothic

Music, geometry and light interpreted in stone and coloured glass are the fundamentals of Gothic architecture. The word Gothic comes from the tribe of Goths, one of those so-called barbarian peoples who infiltrated the Roman Empire in the fifth century. It was originally a term of abuse, in the same way we still use the word vandal, which has the same historic source. The first three things – music, geometry and light – because they were something to do with divine reality and these churches were created to be images of that divine reality.

At root is the doctrine of creation which affirms that God, who is alone eternal, uncreated and of absolute goodness, beauty and truth, creates a world which reflects His own glory. A great deal of the thinking behind the Gothic style of the late twelfth and early thirteenth centuries derived from St Augustine of Hippo. His work, together with the philosophy of Plato, was at the heart of twelfth-century thought.

Alan of Lille described the creation with God as artful architect (*elegans architectus*) who builds the cosmos as His regal palace by the subtle claims of musical consonance. So, let us look at musical theory. A piece of string stretched between two points, when plucked, gives a particular note which we will call C. If the string is held down at half its length then the note, which results from allowing only half of the total to vibrate is a note 8 higher than the original, i.e. C: what is called an octave. So these two are in proportion 1:2. The notes which make a fifth from C and a fourth are in proportion 2:3 and 3:4. These proportions were widely used. For example the nave elevation at Lichfield is 2:1:1; and the arcade itself divided at the capital is 1:1.

This was also seen to have been used in the Old Testament structures. The Temple of Solomon had a length, width and height of 60,20 and 30 cubits and the inner cella, the holy of holies was 20 cubits cubed. Similarly the Ark of Noah was 300 x 50 x 30. The square is the basis of all this: 1:1. The bays of the aisles at Roche Abbey are square and the nave is twice the width of an aisle, and thus half of the overall width. The string course marking the outer walls of the aisles is also the same height as the aisle width. In fact the basic shape of a Gothic elevation can be determined from the square. Geometrical forms, circle, square, were believed to be the rationale behind the creation. In other words, the natural world used these figures and proportions. So, in copying them for its buildings the Church was at once in harmony with the cosmos and with God. Indeed Platonic philosophy, taken up by Augustine, believed that the physical world was only a symbol of reality: the visible reflecting the invisible, but they had no doubt that the absolute reality was that which was invisible. The Church then is a model of the universe and an image of the celestial city. Revelation 21,10f describes the City of God as a square with 12 foundation stones, 12 gates and the walls 144 (i.e. 12 x 12) cubits high and each quarter of the wall is 36 cubits.

Light is also part of John's vision in Revelation. The city shone (21.11), built of pure gold 'bright as clear glass' (21.18), the streets were 'like translucent glass' (21.21). And there is no need for sun or moon for 'the glory of God gave it light, and its lamp was the Lamb' (21.23). So, following the platonic idea, the sources of light in the world are images of the true light of heaven which is God Himself. Light is described in Genesis as the first, vital part of the creative process. 'Let there be light' (Gen 1.3). Indeed light is seen as the creative principle and this is emphasized in St John's Gospel for which the Word 'through whom all things came to be' (John 1.3) is identified as light. 'And the life was the light of men. A light which darkness could never master' (John 1, 4-5). And Jesus proclaims himself as 'the light of the world'.

Light, however, was a created thing but seen as the least material part of creation. Robert Grossesteste (1175-1253) described light as 'the mediator between bodiless and bodily substances, a spiritual body'. From that it is only a small step to see light as the visible form of the invisible divine light. *La luce divina* of Dante

> For God's rays penetrate with shafts so keen
> Through all the universe in due degree
> There's naught can parry them or intervene.
> (*Il Paradiso* XXXI 22-24)

St Bonaventure (c1217-1274) said that amongst corporal things light is most similar to the divine light and he wrote of light in earthly substances as when we polish metal and stone: which is of course, light reflected.

T.S. Eliot in one of his 'Choruses from the Rock'

> We thank thee for the light we have kindled,
> The light of altar and sanctuary;
> all lights of those who meditate at midnight
> And lights directed through the coloured panes of windows
> and light reflected from polished stone,
> the gilden carven wood, the coloured fresco.[2]

English Gothic uses Purbeck stone, commonly called marble, although it isn't. It can be polished and part of the richness which made it popular is the glimmering light on polished stone. Glass itself is made from sand and ash – very material things to make something so transparent.

The master masons conceived ways of making huge windows so that instead of them being openings in the wall of stone, the stone becomes a frame. But unlike Hagia Sophia, where the building is lit by that circle of windows at the base of the dome, and lit with clear light, the medieval churches were lit through coloured glass, as we may still see in York Minster and the Trinity Chapel at Canterbury. But, light of a different sort, clear, and as it happens from the north, is what we get through the huge windows of the Lady Chapel at Ely. Once filled with coloured glass the chapel would have had a sense of mystery. That is gone, but the pure, vibrant light is there now even, perhaps especially, on days when the sun isn't shining. It has a cool quality, and is quite unlike the master mason's vision, but it is glorious none the less.

That was a digression. The writers use the language of light to describe both harmony and architecture: lucid, luminous, clear, so that light is metaphorically at the heart of the creative structure, and musical and visual beauty.

Another writer to rival Augustine was Pseudo-Dionysius. A confusion arose, partly deliberately, by identifying three guys as one. The first was Dionysius of the Areopagitic Court in Acts 17.34. Then there was an anonymous writer from Syria in the late fifth century who gives the impression in his writings that he was in fact the Acts' character, and thirdly, there was St Denis, the third-century apostle of France. This combination of mystical theologian (fifth century) with an apostolic figure (first century) and the founder of French Christianity (third century) was potent and gave these writings an enormous influence, especially in France. This was especially true of the Ile de France, which despite having no architectural tradition of its own – all came from 'abroad', Normandy, Burgundy for example – was to be the birthplace of the new architecture. Pseudo-Dionysius' writing about God, heaven, the angels and the mystery of light was of enormous influence.

Gothic design allowed the maximum infiltration of light: pillars were slimmer and in line with each other, around ambulatories for instance where often they had stood out of line and therefore blocking light. The building was designed from inside, so we have the middle tier of the three storeys much reduced and large windows in both aisles and clerestory. The vaults still need great support, so the buttressing is concentrated and we have flying buttresses and pinnacles. These are invisible from inside. Again, there is something harmonious in the matter of thrust and counter-thrust, in the containment of the essential stresses. A balance is achieved which brings grace and elegance. The light, the height, the proportion, the grace is all as a result of strict geometry and the hidden buttress.

Here we see a fundamental of the spiritual life: rules and structure-creating freedom. 'Whose service is perfect freedom'. The building appears to soar heavenward but it is all downward thrust.

The twelfth century brought a new confidence in the Church and surely without it this prodigious building work – dozens of cathedrals, hundreds of parish churches – would not have been possible. We know from the work of social historians that the Middle Ages could be a time of cruelty, of oppression, of war, of great injustice, but an age that can build structures like Chartres and Lincoln has also a great faith and yet more, a great joy. If faith is the dominant virtue of the Romanesque, then the Gothic speaks of joy and hope. It is upward soaring, it makes us look, there is so much to see, we look upward, hardly aware of our feet. Daniel-Rops describes this as 'supernatural joy'.[3] In a Gothic building there is a physical sensation which evokes the spiritual: vast areas of light, brilliance of form and structure, draw us out of ourselves to find glory. Romanesque is about an inner life; Gothic gives strength to the inner through the impressions of sight and sound around us.

The cathedrals of France have immense height: the vault at Chartres is 131' and Amiens is 138'. Beauvais reached 157' but it did collapse. England's by contrast are relatively low: Lichfield only 57', Wells 67', Lincoln 82'. Which stand comparison with the Romanesque: Ely 72' and Durham 73'. Only Westminster Abbey, one of the most French buildings in England, emulates the French at 102'. But because we were not too ambitious in height of vaults, we could not only build long, but also have towers and spires unheard of in the Ile de France. We shall return to them later.

The varieties of Gothic in England are many. Each cathedral has its own distinct character. The stone is different, the overall designs are unique in almost every case, and the details always so. Those buildings erected in this new style from about 1170 through to 1250, say, have a freshness, a sense of vigour and vitality that still addresses us eight centuries later. Once more I leave you to discover the joys and excitements.

CHAPTER XXI

Late Gothic

G othic architecture is often divided into three periods: Early English, Decorated and Perpendicular. The spiritual foundation remains fundamentally the same, with the light through huge windows, geometry, height, vaulting, weight and thrust concealed. Learning to recognize the different styles and so to be able to work out the details of changes in a building is one of the joys of church looking. And looking at the details, bosses, carvings, glass can be a life-long activity. I leave you to find out all that and to have fun.

Many churches did have major changes sometimes involving complete rebuildings. Older structures were given new vaults, towers and spires were raised high above the roofs. And within there were additions of screens, chantry chapels and enrichment of furnishings. Such rebuildings and additions continued well into the sixteenth century. Bell Harry, the great central tower in Canterbury, was begun in 1496. The towers at Durham were completed about 1500. The Norwich spire is of c1480 and the vaulting of the cathedral continued into the next century. The fan-vaulted retroquire at Peterborough was built from 1496 to 1508. Ripon's nave is early sixteenth century and Bath Abbey was completely rebuilt in the years 1500-1530 and not really finished when surrendered to the King in January 1539. The story is told in greater detail later.

There was still a vitality about the English Church, a desire to beautify. The masons were developing further their ideas and we see the outcome in fan-vaults and pendants. Among the cathedrals, Oxford is the one to visit. The history is complicated. It was originally an Augustinian priory housing the shrine of the eighth-century saint, Frideswide. Cardinal Wolsey suppressed the priory in order to create Cardinal College and he lopped off part of the nave to make a great courtyard. He planned, and indeed started, a new chapel so the whole was eventually to have been demolished. Interestingly the presbytery vault had only been built about 1500 – more of that in a moment, but to complete the story: Wolsey fell from grace in 1529 and Henry took over the college project. The buildings are still profuse with cardinals' hats but it became known as Christ Church. Henry kept the priory church, now become college chapel, to be the cathedral of a new diocese in 1546.

The eastern arm is fascinating. The east wall is by Scott in the nineteenth century, but the rest is medieval. The circular romanesque piers have the 'gallery' tucked under the arches. Above, a string course has shafts running down through it to the capitals of the arcade, and above, the clerestory, is panelled and then there is the vault. The vault proper is in squares but the bays are not, so borrowing a technique from the carpenters' hammer-beam structure, the mason constructed arches across the width into which the vault fits, the arch joining the vault to the walls via the panelling. At the point where the vault meets the arch are pendants. They work like keystones, their weight actually strengthening the whole structure. The mason who devised this was probably William Orchard. It is interesting to compare this with Orchard's vaulting in the Divinity School in Oxford of 1480-3 and then the vault of the Henry VII Chapel at Westminster built a bit later.

What Oxford shows is that new things were still being created. A smallish community was able to transform its church in the most glorious way. Gothic architecture was in fact reaching its late wondrous phase but had the Reformation not happened who is to say that fan-vaulting would have been its culmination? Without that upheaval there might have been yet further developments.

I think this asks us to be prepared always for the new and exciting. Life can continue with fresh vigour of spirit even into old age, if we are expectant of the new and the beautiful. Technology moves on and we move with it. The vaulting in Oxford also reminds us yet again that each age has its own style reaching forward and upwards. Our greater churches constantly point to this. When a tower collapses or a community decides to enhance its church then we find an Ely Octagon or the lierne vaults at Norwich, Bell Harry at Canterbury or the west facade of Peterborough, which is unlike both the nave that lies behind it, or the porch that was added to it in the fourteenth century.

Rarely is a church all of one style. Each addition is innovative, creative, in the forefront and we only lost our nerve in the nineteenth century. Despite Coventry, and Liverpool Metropolitan we haven't yet regained it. It will take a resurgence of Christian faith to do that. The Church in Europe is old and needs renewal but perhaps that has already begun and in the future we may see the Church employing the new architecture when it builds or rebuilds.

CHAPTER XXII

Reformation

The religious changes of the sixteenth century were tumultuous. It is difficult to grasp the various views, theological and political, for they were so fluid. Men changed their minds, their thoughts developed and the drive of political power was remorseless. It was an age of polemic and no-one was not partisan. Even today the stance from which one writes colours one's views of the period.

Liturgically there was a radical, and yet conservative, revision. The vernacular was to be used but the Eucharist and Daily Office, though much shorn, remained.

And at what point do we try to freeze the past to examine it? Throughout the period from the 1520s, when Henry's need for divorce from Katherine of Aragon was of great urgency, through to 1662 and the publication of the revised Book of Common Prayer following the Restoration of Charles II, there was constant change. The theological views of princes and their advisors bring periods of protestant ascendancy, of catholic restoration, of persecution, of king at war with Parliament, of Puritan rule, and the final settlement of Charles II had distinct features from those of Elizabeth I and that golden age of Anglican writing and liturgy in the first three decades of the seventeenth century; those whom we call the Caroline divines.

Much that we see now, or rather much that we do not see in the greater churches, comes from this period. The destruction of glass, of statues, of chantries, shrines, altars, screens was part of the Reformation's zeal, either in the immediate period of Edward VI's reign or under Cromwell. And all but the poorest of churches will have been refurnished, if not re-ordered, several times over since then. Only with the twentieth century liturgical renaissance did most of our greater churches begin to rediscover the colour, the order, the beauty of the medieval years. Yet we are not medievalists and we do not go back.

One feature of the Reformation in England was its ruthless quality. Henry VIII simply dissolved all the monasteries. In some countries it was agreed that the monastic life was mistaken and therefore had open policies to encourage monks and nuns to return to secular life. But in some countries the system was allowed to expire naturally. One convent in Maribo in Denmark didn't finally close until 1621. But in England suppression was the way, although under a pretence of non-compulsion. Houses actually surrendered to the King. In fact between 1536 and 1540 all monastic houses were surrendered. Their lands, under an Act of 1539, were vested in the Crown, but the Crown, always short of cash, soon sold or leased them, and this financial element seems to have been uppermost in the King's mind. For this was also to be true of the dissolution of the Chantries in 1545; the revenues went to the Crown. Henry planned to 'save' sixteen monasteries: eight were the monastic cathedrals which we refounded, but with far fewer members of the foundation. Six were to become new cathedrals and two became colleges: these latter, at Burton and Thornton, lasted for five and seven years respectively. The great gatehouse at Thornton still stands not far from the Humber, in north Lincolnshire. Some 15 per cent of monastic wealth was 'salvaged' for the Church. But the only permanent piece of genuine salvage was the five bishoprics. There had been no new sees in England since the creation of Carlisle in 1133. There is a list in the King's own hand linking 19 counties (12 in pairs) with the names of 21 houses. But this is more about revenues than buildings.

The new cathedrals were to be at Gloucester, Chester, Peterborough, Bristol, Oseney (just to the west of Oxford) and Westminster. Oseney was soon exchanged for Christ Church in Oxford, and Westminster was a cathedral for only ten years and under Elizabeth became the Royal Peculiar – the Collegiate Church of St Peter. All the new foundations were more modest than their predecessors. At Norwich the prior became the first dean, but only five monks were retained as prebendaries, together with sixteen petty canons. Durham had a dean, eleven canons and an unspecified number of petty canons. A number of places had students but these were soon abolished. This process of slimming down the cathedral foundations continued at intervals until the present day. Today the number of clerics is small, rarely more than dean and three canons and perhaps one or two minor canons, but the numbers of lay people employed has risen enormously: administrators, people concerned with the fabric, shops, restaurants, visitors' officers and so on.

Of other greater churches several were bought by the local community and became parish churches. The monastic buildings were mainly demolished except in places where new foundations were created: Durham and Ely as examples and we have noted those in looking at precincts.

This revolution in the life of the Church was carried through with hardly a word of dissent. There was indeed the Pilgrimage of Grace in the North which resulted in defeat and the deaths of six heads of houses. But as Dom David Knowles observes they mostly went with no argument accepting 'rich prizes for the abandonment alike of the service of God which they had vowed and of the flock for whom they were responsible'.[1]

The story of Bath Abbey may briefly be told. Oliver King became Bishop of Bath and Wells in 1495 and when he visited Bath in 1499 he found the building in ruinous condition. He had a vision of a rebuilt church which included Jacob's Ladder. The nave was demolished, the eastern arm abandoned and a new cruciform church built on the site of the nave. King died in 1503 but his new abbey continued to be built into the 1530s. The abbey surrendered in January 1539 and the city was offered the church for 500 marks. However, they turned it down. The lead was stripped off the roofs and it looked as if the abbey church would be destroyed. In 1548 Matthew Colthurst bought it and his son, having restored it, gave it to the city in 1572. But the building still remained incomplete. Indeed the nave wasn't properly roofed until early in the next century. It is one of that group of very fine late Gothic buildings; the proportion of window to masonry is 6:1. The vaults are plaster and were put up by Scott in 1869.

On Mary's accession the secular chapter at Westminster was dissolved on 27 September 1556, and by November sixteen monks, who had volunteered, were installed. Dr Feckenham, the Dean of St Paul's was elected Abbot. He had been a monk at Evesham but had spent most of Edward VI's reign in the Tower. He set to work to re-establish Westminster as a Benedictine Abbey. St Edward's shrine was rebuilt and the Confessor's body restored to it. However, Mary's reign was short and she was buried in the abbey only four years after her coronation. The funeral was to be followed within a month by the coronation of Elizabeth I. The abbot was offered the see of Canterbury but he refused. He was not prepared to follow the new ways. The monks were again dispersed but Feckenham wasn't hurried out. He left the abbey in May 1560 to enter the Tower, once more a prisoner. He lived for a further twenty-four years, years spent in various places either in prison or under house arrest, until his death in 1584. At that time he was immured in Wisbech Castle and he is buried in an unknown grave in the nearby churchyard of St Peter and St Paul.

That so many great buildings could be allowed to fall into ruin, or to be rebuilt as houses reveals the sixteenth century's views of medieval architecture. If they survived it was by chance. Many fell into ruin, or only parts of them remained.

The cloisters, sleeping quarters, refectory, kitchens are gone. Often large parts of the church itself have gone too. In many places only the nave survived, although more rarely, just the eastern arm. It is interesting working out what has survived and what it might have been like once.

Perhaps a typical example is at Crowland. St Guthlac's remote fenland monastery is still remote. The fen landscape, so empty, is formed by dykes and fields, and the ever-present, constantly changing sky. There is a sense of nowhere, and yet of course it is a place where people live. The marsh, sky, reed-bed and open fields make the beyond far off – the opposite of a line of demarcation. At the centre was the great abbey and the lost community is spoken of by the sculptures of the west facade. That and the north aisle, now the parish church, is all that survives. The once elaborate west front tell us much of the past. Pointers that this now small church was once so much greater. There are hints of an earlier spirituality.

Christians in England are constantly being reminded of a past greatness, of a past quite different from the present. Crowland's west front, rather than being part of a church with a spiritual message, is now medieval architecture to be conserved.[2]

Adaption was a key word of these changes. People's lives were altered and buildings kept only if they could be found a new use. People adapted themselves to the realities of the time. A number went to their deaths: burnings were not uncommon in Elizabeth's reigns as well as those of Henry VIII, Edward VI and Mary. Some spent long years imprisoned, but the majority went with the wind and perhaps hoped for better days. A similar response came in the next century when following the defeat and execution of Charles I the Church went underground. It survived in the end because of Charles II's restoration, and if that had not happened history would have been very different.

Sister Elizabeth Ruth Obard writing about Walsingham, another place destroyed by the Reformation, says, 'this devastation had a purifying effect'. Walsingham like ravaged Jerusalem slept among the ruins. Wealth, questionable relics, pilgrimages of dubious repute, 'all the abuses attendant on a religious community that has an over-abundance of life's good things' these were causes for change.[3] The centuries pass and now there is a new resurgence of prayer, peace, understanding based on simplicity, humility that are born of respect for others. This is true of Walsingham and perhaps of many other places. The problems so many greater churches now face are from the need for money, and their success as places people want to visit. The visitors, as with so many other attractions, like National Parks, for instance, are in danger of destroying the very thing that attracts them in the first place. Most places have restaurants and shops, by far the majority outside the church itself. They provide for sale things people want and it all helps to pay the bills. I wonder though if it might be possible to find ways of using the places spiritually, and actually making some money out of that too. Why should we not pay for a day workshop on prayer, for example, just as we pay for a guide book or a meal?

When we visit ruins, or churches mere fragments of their former selves, we bring with us who we are today. I come as an Anglican, culturally, historically, deeply so, and yet increasingly alienated from the Church of today. Others will come with very different preoccupations, but the question we all face is about how the present and the past mesh, and how we look into the future. This is not only a question about the past of the Church, but also about our own past. How do we carry that, which we may regret, into the present?

The dome of St Paul's once dominated the skyline of London. Now it competes, not very successfully, with the high-rise office blocks. Finance is clearly more important than religion.

A rare opportunity to see the eighteenth-century paving in the nave at York.
Usually the nave is full of chairs.

Sir Edwin Lutyens planned this huge basilica for Liverpool, but only the crypt was built.

Standing on a part of the crypt is the Metropolitan Cathedral of Liverpool. It's modern tower vies on the skyline with the massive tower of the Anglican Cathedral. Two twentieth-century statements about the Church in Liverpool, and reminding us forceably of Christian disunity.

The huge tapestry of Christ in Majesty by Graham Sutherland dominates the interior of Sir Basil Spence's Cathedral at Coventry. It speaks powerfully of the triumphant love of God for his people in Christ's victory over death.

The central portion of Portsmouth Cathedral is focussed on lectern and altar – Word and Sacrament – and beyond is the Chapel of St Thomas calling us on in our earthly journey toward God.

This is the spire that they dared to build in Salisbury. It is a strong image of the striving upward of Christian faith, calling us beyond our reach.

The Chapel of St Blaise at Lincoln with wall paintings by Duncan Grant, completed in 1958.

Peter Ball's sculpture is extremely compelling. It hangs above the pulpit in the Octagon at Ely.

Modern-day monks in the Quire at Buckfast Abbey in Devon. This is a place where you can see what many of our greater churches were once like – the place of worship of a living monastic community.

CHAPTER XXIII

St Paul's Cathedral

Only one great church was built from the end of the Middle Ages until the nineteenth century and that was St Paul's, the cathedral of London. Inigo Jones had made some repairs and alterations to the old cathedral in the 1630s but after the Great Fire of 1666 the decision was made to clear the site and Sir Christopher Wren was appointed to design the new cathedral. For the first time the reformed but catholic Church of England could build a cathedral. It is hard now to imagine the shock of the new style. There were already some classical churches but to create a great classical cathedral in the heart of the capital was to speak volumes about the attitude Restoration London had to its medieval past.

Cathedrals had always been built in the latest style and classicism provided an apt vehicle for the pride of the City of London. Here was to be a church for solemn occasions. Wren, the polymath whose principle interests had been in mathematics, physics and astronomy, now turned to architecture. He built with a cool grandeur. The cathedral is detached and aloof. However, the plan is essentially medieval: nave, quire, crossing and the internal arrangements were more conservative than they now are. The high altar was in the eastern apse (now a small chapel) and the quire had returned stalls set against a screen with the organ above. That desire for long vistas had not yet arisen. Here was a church with great spaces for ceremony – that under the dome being a triumph, but the enclosed quire is for the sung opus Dei as always. Altars were few. The Eucharist, although central to worship, was not a frequent event. This is a church for preaching. So we can see in it many of the characteristics of Restoration Anglicanism.

The Book of Common Prayer, which was revised in 1662, and the Authorised Version of the Bible were central. There was a purity, a reason and this is a spirituality of recollection. The drama is extremely restrained. All is internal, emotion is controlled. It is a style that hardly needs images.

There are festoons, the wrought-ironwork of Tijou, the carvings of Gibbons and Jonathan Mayne by way of decoration, but the mosaics are much later and more Baroque excess than faithful to Wren. Something of the natural world is there but tamed, a mere exhibit. Thomas Traherne, one of the great mystical writers of the age, gloried in the natural world but it led to a right appreciation of the deep mystery of the Cross. His eyes were fixed on the happiness to which the Cross admits us. There is a reasonable conviction of salvation, undemonstrative, built up from perceptions of the natural and well as the divine law.

Churches, shrines, holy places were important but here is a sobriety as far removed from medieval catholicism as from the rollicking life of Restoration London which would be satirized by Hogarth and others in the next century. The Church was deeply moral and the architecture's round-headed arches, its dignity in fluted columns and Corinthian capitals reflects the divine but also humane order of a Christian morality.

Apart from the detached red-brick Chapter House, there were no ancillary buildings. The 'corners' of the design were sufficient for vestries, library and consistory court, for this building housed a liturgy that was bare and simple.

The cathedral rose dramatically above the roofs of London and was the dominant focus among the many towers and spires that were being built by Wren and others at the same time. Much of the money for this grand rebuilding scheme came from a tax on coal. This was as much a state venture as a church one, but a state in which the Church remained a vital force. How things have changed. The planners and architects of the 1960s put an end to Wren's skyline. London, long the centre of world finance, became a city of tall towers in glass, steel and concrete. Many views of St Paul's do remain but the Christian landscape has gone. One cannot but see in this a reflection of the role of the Church in society today. The Church provides bases of calm and peace in the turmoil and stresses of the financial markets rather than centres of inspiration that direct the life of the City. There remains, however, the civic pride and the institutions of the City continue to maintain, to repair and beautify the City churches. Plans to close many met with strong resistance and have been thwarted, and among them all is the cathedral, grand, dignified, cool, not calling attention to itself but waiting to be found. Engaged with the secular life around it but now more on the edges, marginalized, trying to find a role. A church inspired by the faith of men like Hooker, Lancelot Andrewes, or Traherne which combined the public, the ordered, the formal with a deep personal piety. That contrast is there in St Paul's.

Jeremy Taylor in his Episcopal Charge of 1661 spoke with urgency. 'By preaching and catechizing, and private intercourse all the needs of souls can best be served.' And he didn't say it, for it was known by all, but the context is always daily worship: Morning and Evening Prayer, psalms, chunks of Scripture to be weighed, canticles, prayers. The BCP is still in use. Its language is formal and rich yet also restrained. It matches the Baroque architecture, but it isn't of our age. To my mind the classical Anglicanism of the seventeenth and eighteenth centuries is much further removed from today than is the medieval period.

St Paul's has an element of illusion, despite its apparent simple openness. The facade with its two-storey elevation matches nothing within, and the upper storey of the rest is make-believe. The windows are blank, and behind this screen are the flying buttresses. It is as if the mechanics must not be seen. However, the wall forms a podium for the dome. Each element of that has the effect of 'lift': base, drum, attic and lantern are all taller in proportion to the cupola than those of that other great dome at St Peter's in Rome. Michelangelo's is in stone, Wren's in lead and wood. And in London the inner dome is not what we see from outside. A brick cone carries the cupola and this is hidden by the inner dome. In fact here are three structures. In this regard St Paul's is an act of theatre – an illusion behind a proscenium arch, and it works. 'An Anglican O altitudo', wrote Pevsner.[1]

St Paul's is, next to Westminster Abbey, the place of burial and memorial of the 'great and the good'. We find it hard to distinguish the Christian virtues amidst the wordly success – military, imperial, commercial. I find all this marble hard to take.

What does St Paul's say to us today? I believe it calls us to ask questions about how our 'religious' life relates to the rest of life. If religion is to be real it must colour the whole of life. How does our church-going, our prayer and devotions sit with our family, our work, our interests? Are they like St Paul's, marginalized on the edges, because the pursuit of worldly goals and ambitions is paramount? Do the successes of technology, of commerce, of industry choke our spiritual nature?

For me that dome surrounded by the great towers also asks how does the Church speak to the world of the rich, without fatally damaging its own integrity and morality. How does success in this world's terms relate to the Gospel? I work in the North in parishes which are disadvantaged, with the social problems that come from poverty and exclusion so I have no experience of these things, but I do ask the question.

CHAPTER XXIV

The Eighteenth and Nineteenth Centuries

Alec Clifton-Taylor says that the 'cathedrals probably suffered less from iconoclasm than from sheer neglect'.[1] Gothic style was out of fashion in the seventeenth and eighteenth centuries: it lacked the symmetry and balance that was all the rage. Anglican liturgy of the BCP plain and unadorned didn't fit the medieval buildings, with their multiplicity of chapels and long naves. You have only to see how little used are the lesser spaces of Beverley Minster, for example, by a churchmanship not really at home with a medieval building.

By the later eighteenth century, however, interest was renewed by the need for major repair. On Easter Monday 1786 the west tower of Hereford Cathedral collapsed. James Wyatt was brought in by the Dean and Chapter and he worked there for the next eight years. Wyatt took down the whole Romanesque west bay and so reduced the length of the nave. He also removed everything above the arcades and then rebuilt. His work calls forth various responses. Pevsner calls it self-effacing but his west facade didn't survive.[2] This was demolished and rebuilt by John Oldrid Scott in 1904-8. Pevsner clearly did not like this. He described the detail as vociferous and wondered why Scott had felt it necessary to introduce a full-blown decorated style. On the whole Wyatt is now castigated for his work although, of course, it was always done at the behest of, and with the approval of, the deans and chapters. It was they who decided to shorten the Hereford nave, but even in his own time Wyatt earned the nickname the Destroyer.

Attitudes change. Fashions come and go and different generations with varying philosophies and beliefs also come and go. Nowadays the talk is of conservation rather than restoration but often that seems to me to err on the side of maintaining an historic artefact rather than continuing the tradition of making things new.

I suppose we tend to do that because of what we deem to be the errors of the past – especially Wyatt, but also other 'restorers', even those as scholarly as Sir Gilbert Scott. Salisbury Cathedral employed Wyatt too from 1789. He wanted to create a long vista so removed all the screens to open up the entire length of the cathedral. He positioned the high altar in the Trinity Chapel. This is completely at odds with the design of the building and although the high altar is back where it should be only a wrought-iron screen is there to the east of it, and the view is still unimpeded from the west doors to the east wall. Symmetry and balance were all, so Wyatt moved medieval monuments and placed them on plinths between the nave arcades. Outside he changed the ground levels to create a great landscape. The cathedral sits in its park like a great country house. It is all elegance and panorama. Constable's paintings of a generation later have imprinted this style on our imagination and now for better or worse, and I tend to think for better, Salisbury is a medieval cathedral in an Augustan setting. But his interior depredations could be put right. What an opportunity for a contemporary architect to design new screens. The shrine of St Osmund could be returned to the retroquire and the other monuments replaced.

Lord Burlington and William Kent laid a new floor in York Minster about 1731-5 and thus destroyed all the medieval tombs. It is in black and white marble. The *Church Times* published a photograph on 2 February 1996 showing the nave empty so as to expose this design. The nave had been empty until the 1860s when, first benches and then chairs, were introduced to seat those who came to the nave services initiated by the Dean. Now, the nave is nearly always full of chairs and nave sanctuary furniture. Surely this might be removed for most of the winter months?

Walpole and Gray were among the few eighteenth-century people to appreciate medieval architecture and by the mid-nineteenth century their influence had helped to create a different climate of opinion. Restoration rather than destruction and rebuilding became the order of the day. But what did people mean by restoration'? Did it involve replacing what had been there but destroyed by time or disaster? How much change was permitted?

Chester, built of sandstone, was always going to need much attention due to the effects of weather and even nineteenth-century air pollution. It is a good place to see what happened in terms of restoration. Thomas Harrison (1818-20) and Richard Hussey (1843-64) did some minor work but when Scott inspected the cathedral in 1868 he described it as a smouldering sandstone cliff. Urgent and major work was required.[3] He rebuilt the top of the tower and planned to add a spire, but this was never executed. The plan, however, shows that Scott was not content with merely replacing what was already there. The quire clerestory, the flying buttresses to both south transept and nave, the west front battlements are all his work. Internally he vaulted the quire (with Clayton and Bell adding decoration), and also vaulted the nave and aisles. His 'daring conceit'[4] was the polygonal roof at the east end of the south aisle. He claimed that this had been the original design but that has always been questioned. Sir George's work covered 1868-76. Next on the scene was Sir Arthur Blomfield who repaired and restored St Werburgh's shrine (it has had further work more recently), and inserted the south window of the south transept. His son, Charles, took over from him in 1900-2 and rebuilt the south transept vault. Sir Giles Scott became architect from 1908 and added fan vaults to the south-west porch and replaced the east window of the refectory.

All this is about our attitude to the past. In England, despite the Reformation and Commonwealth, and the mistakes of earlier restorers, we have an extremely rich inheritance. We are rightly proud of this, but we are in danger of living in the past. Our economic life, once centred on manufacturing, has changed almost beyond recognition. There are new industries, there is the enormous growth in financial and other service industries but wherever you go there are new 'heritage' venues growing up. I worry about all this and the way in which we package the past for people. Museums use so many modern techniques to help people understand the past, but in doing so they are imposing our view of what the past was like. No longer do we simply display what we have of the past, but it has to be active. People dress up, sound is provided and even smells. A few of our greater churches have taken steps down this track. Often in the shops rather than in the church itself. But I have been to churches where music is piped through. Usually inappropriate music, but the authorities think they are helping people to understand the building better, whereas in fact they are doing the opposite: they destroy the peace and silence which is the real meaning of the building. We need to help people understand the origins of these places – that's a prime purpose of this book – but not at the cost of today. If people come to see a living church they must be helped to enter into its present meaning. That meaning can be enhanced by understanding origins and roots but it is of today. I long to see something of our own age in the building itself. Furnishings usually are in evidence: there are many new windows (glass therein, I mean) and altar frontals, vestments and so on. But we miss other opportunities, or is it that the authorities would never allow it to be done? The north outer aisle at Chichester has had all the window tracery replaced. You can tell this because of the new colour of the stone, whereas it takes a discerning eye to tell medieval from nineteenth-century copy. The copies then were usually machine tooled; now we do it by hand, as the medieval masons did. When Chichester's stone has weathered it will be impossible to tell that this isn't medieval. Why could we not have new, modern design tracery in these windows, something that would tell the observer in 2098 that this was done a century ago?

Heritage and conservation is leading to mock medieval buildings: they look medieval but are actually late twentieth century. At least the Victorians had the courage to be themselves, as we will see in another chapter.

CHAPTER XXV

The Nineteenth and Twentieth Centuries

The changes since 1800 in how we live and in the mental furniture with which we confront the world have been enormous. The upward curve of the rate of technological change is steep indeed. In a book of this kind I can only sketch these changes with bold sweeps of my brush. In 1800 people lived in rural communities and even towns and cities had the air of the countryside. In politics the reforms of the 1830s led to universal suffrage and eventually to the constitutional reforms of the 1990s. The social changes deriving from the political and economic changes of the 1945 Labour government and the Conservative one of 1979 are still evident. The confident, progressive ideals of the nineteenth century crumpled under the horrors of two world wars, the economic depression between them, and then the Cold War and the nuclear arms race. The apparent triumph of capitalism leaves us at the beginning of a new millennium with insufficient funding of health and education here, and with continued deprivation and poverty in large areas of the world. The environmental issues continue to confront us and the political will to make real inroads into the problems is not forthcoming.

The scientific advances are very considerable. I suppose the key one has been the influence of Darwin's work. His *Origin of Species* and the work of early geologists and psychologists has torn apart the fabric of religious faith in the Western world. Science, politics, social change – all have driven religious faith into defensive postures.

The modern world knows it is adrift and yet for most people the answers which religion once provided are no means of finding anchorage. All has been tried. Religion is revealed as phoney, and mankind is lost in a godless world. Wagner's *Gotterdämerung* has come to be.

Against this religion can retreat. It can take to the bunkers, hide behind ditches, become fundamentalist, beleaguered but defiant. And we see much of this approach. It has its attractions. Alternatively, and mainstream Christianity seeks to do this, it upholds the faith but does so by being engaged in dialogue. It goes on trying to show the validity of the Gospel but equally does not ignore the problems, the alienations of the secular world, for if the world is to return to faith those issues must be addressed.

Some of that secular world tries to write off Christianity and our buildings and ceremonies. They want to relegate them to history and heritage. So we are encouraged to enjoy our Christian heritage but not as a living faith. Rather as an exhibit in a museum. I am astonished by the number of churches which feel it necessary to inform visitors that these places are in use by living communities of faith. That suggests a lack of confidence by the Church as well as a recognition of the ignorance of many visitors.

I believe the Church must help the modern world explore its pain, its alienation, the brutality and emptiness of so much human experience. In terms of buildings and works of art that is hard, for religious buildings and art start from a different perspective. The great works of art of the last century or so try both to describe the experience and also to interpret and seek for meaning. I think for instance of the symphonies of Mahler and Shostakovich. Music, because of its spiritual language, is able to do that in ways which other art forms, especially those using words, find hard or impossible. Often Christian works do not start from the human perception but simply confront the listener, the observer with the Gospel. I can see why, but that is part of the problem for the world believes the Gospel to be unrelated to its concerns. It appears more as a fairy story which has lost its hold. In a world like ours the achievements of Messiaen, Rouault, Epstein, of Sutherland, of D.L. Sayers and T.S. Eliot are of extraordinary value. But only rarely in the twentieth century have there been expressions of truth that ring with confidence, hope and love.

Our great churches by their very nature are unable to describe the human condition. The older they are in some ways the less connected they become, for they enable those who can to find comfort in them, in the past, because they ignore the present, and therefore let those people off the hook of trying to speak to the modern world. What we need are the means of helping those folk to engage with the God of hope who comes to us from the future.

As we have already observed the Church has lost its nerve and only in small ways, although almost everywhere, is it able quietly and confidently to continue. There are many saplings, but few mature trees.

In the last hundred years the Church has begun the process of renewal. It has made false starts, it has stumbled and still struggles to find ways of helping itself and others to feed from the truth it guards and nurtures.

Some of this has been in the commissioning of new buildings and works of art and of those more further on, but for the moment a little more about renewal.

Liturgical renewal goes back to tentative beginnings in the nineteenth century. In England the pressure for reform of the Book of Common Prayer came from both evangelicals, wishing to remove the last vestiges of Catholicism, and from the growing Anglo-Catholic movement with its return to older customs – candles, cross, vestments.

A Royal Commission of 1867-70 led to a lectionary revision in 1871 and the Public Worship Regulation Act of 1874 under which prosecutions were brought, including that against the Bishop of Lincoln, Edward King. A further Royal Commission on Ecclesiastical Discipline sat from 1904 and in its report of 1906 acknowledged that the BCP was 'too narrow for the religious life of the present generation'. Change came extremely slowly. The revised BCP of 1927 and 1928 was twice rejected by Parliament, but then published with tacit episcopal approval for its use.

Meanwhile on the continent the Benedictines had been at the forefront of liturgical renewal in the Roman Church and amazingly, it seems, as early as 1903 an encyclical *Motu proprio* of Pope Pius X set the movement forward. 'Active participation ... is the primary indispensable source of a true Christian Spirit,' wrote the Pope. Hebert in his extremely influential book of 1935 goes on to say that renewal was 'to recall the faithful to the treasures which they possess in the liturgy and to realise anew the ancient ideal of Christian worship as the common prayer of the Church, the act of the whole Body, in which all members have a part'.[1]

Rome finally moved with the Second Vatican Council (1962-5) and the Church of England made a conservative and what now seems hesitant start to reform in the mid-1960s too. Changing rites and even reordering churches is only a start. The people of God have to grasp their role and the underlying theology. The new services and rearrangements of furniture were not always well taught to the congregations. The position of the altar was the principle change. It was 'to revive the ancient Roman practice of so arranging the altar that the priest can stand on the far side of it facing the people, with the express object of bringing the people more in touch with the liturgical action'.

However, no degree of liturgical change would transform the Church unless it also became outward looking. Hebert again:

> If the modern world [remember, please, he was published in 1935] regards Christianity as the special concern of the religiously minded, and therefore leaves it on one side, it is because Christians themselves have set the example . . . When modern religion instead of claiming for God and transforming the whole of social life, including the schoolboy's football and the shopkeeper's profits, leaves these on one side and limits itself to the life of piety lived by the devout, the principle of the Incarnation is lost.

And that has often been the continuing problem, but let me now come on to the greater churches of these two centuries.

The Roman Catholic Church built many new cathedrals, but these are nearly all parochial in status and structure. There is neither complexity of building nor lavish resourcing. Two cathedrals funded by the Duke of Norfolk, in Norwich and Arundel (1870-3 and 1882-1910) and that in Westminster (1895-1903) are the exceptions. The more recent Metropolitan Cathedral in Liverpool is too, but the recent ones in Clifton and Brentwood are borderline cases. The Church of England, despite enormous increases in population, had created no new dioceses from 1546 until 1836 when the urban Leeds became the population centre of the new diocese of Ripon. That decision itself says a lot. In mid-nineteenth-century England it was fine to place a cathedral in a market town rather than in a populous city simply because there was a cathedral-like building there. Recently the diocesan title has been changed to Ripon and Leeds. The Church did however build new cathedrals in four places: Truro, Liverpool, Guildford and Coventry. All the other new dioceses had parish churches designated as cathedrals although of these Southwell, St Alban's and Southwark had greater churches and Manchester a collegiate one; that again is a borderliner. The others, Newcastle, Bradford, Wakefield, Blackburn and Sheffield in the northern province, and St Edmundsbury and Ipswich (and what does that title say about the Church?),[2] Derby, Chelmsford, Birmingham and Portsmouth in the South. Most of the parish church cathedrals have made alterations and additions with various degrees of success, or rather lack of it. The only one in my view that has become significant is Portsmouth. I begin our survey in Liverpool.

Liverpool was a city of the Empire. Its eight miles of docks and its great mixture of people made it a place of world importance. Trade was the hub of empire and the city has the great Victorian buildings of shipping and commerce. The twentieth century hasn't been kind to the city. Unemployment, dereliction, some degree of regeneration, but a shrinkage of population give it an air of a place that has lost its former splendour. But it was also the swinging city of the 1960s: the home of the Beatles and many other household names of popular music and entertainment. The two cathedrals near to each other on high ground to the south of the city centre reflect the times of their creation. As individuals we relate to our age, shaped by its influences, and the Church although with a timeless Gospel is moulded too by the general attitudes and the march of events. In the Middle Ages it was the prime mover, the persuader, but since the sixteenth century, and increasingly, we respond, often very belatedly and obliquely to the secular world of our day.

The Anglican Cathedral is huge, powerful, heavy and yet borne heavenward. For me it is a mark of Victorian England. It was designed by a young man at the turn of the century. (Both his father and grandfather had designed cathedrals – Edinburgh and Norwich RC.) It isn't, as so many people allege, Gothic Revival although it has deep Gothic roots. One thinks of Albi and the Flamboyant and Spanish Gothic styles but this could only be English and Edwardian. A product of a nation holding sway in the world – a country of great confidence and material power. The concept is grandiose and it took over seventy years to complete. That also tells us of change and tradition. It often took a long time to build a cathedral and war and economic collapse played their part in earlier centuries too. Those built quickly like Salisbury and Chartres are rare. But 1978, when Liverpool was completed, is hardly represented in the building. It's glass, however, does tell the story of the century. Some was replaced after war damage but the changing styles from east to west reveal the changing styles, although the west window on the Benedicite is hardly the most modern of its time. The final note is struck by Elizabeth Frink's Christ above the great west doors: in green bronze, against the red stone it is effective and has a searching quality.

The Roman Catholic cathedral, the mother church of a vast archdiocese, took a long time to come to birth. The diocese was founded in 1850 and it is evidence of its relative poverty that its cathedral wasn't consecrated until 1967. It is a three-part story. Sir Edwin Lutyens' design for a great classical cathedral in white stone was only built at crypt level. It was to have been another example of British imperial grandeur, larger and higher than any other, in a monumental style. A style totally at variance with Scott's but speaking the same language: the Church triumphant, glorious and beating in architectural terms the new 'cathedrals', railway sheds, government buildings, town halls, sports arenas. The crypt building is higher than the normal-size buildings on the streets nearby. It reveals in its massiveness something of the scale that Lutyens had envisioned. It was to have been the kind of building he had created in India to celebrate the Raj.

A cathedral was finally built and that is the second part of the tale. This is a church taking Vatican II seriously. One that is exciting, innovative both in design and structure. The cathedral speaks to us of the 1960s – glass, concrete, steel – centred on the altar. It is a church open to the fresh winds of *aggianormento*, the spring-cleaning wind let in by John XXIII's summoning of the Council . This is a cathedral not about hierarchy, but about the pilgrim people of God. Everyone is only a few yards from the altar.

The third stage is now. The cathedral is spending several times as much money as the original cost to repair the roof, the ribs and the lantern. The surrounds are still rough and makeshift. The stone cladding is discoloured. The whole thing looks dated, rather shabby. Inside is a different story. You enter through automatic doors (well this was the late twentieth century) and find yourself in a place soaked with prayer. It has a numinous quality. It is rather dark and electricity is needed even on sunny days. The uses of the building have changed from the original idea. Many of the surrounding 'chapels' are put to different uses. One, for example, houses a sculpture by Sean Rice called Abraham, a wonderful statement of Christian faith. My feeling is that the suffering of Christ comes close to the suffering of Liverpool in this place.

Guildford take us back in time. A competition was held in 1932 which 183 architects entered – building cathedrals is obviously something architects want to do. Sir Edward Maufe's design was chosen. The foundation stone was laid in 1936 but the war caused a break from 1939 to 1952 and the building was finally consecrated in May 1961. It is basically a medieval design taking no notice whatever of liturgical change. I find it very disappointing. The site is excellent but the building is a kind of watered-down Gothic, to me a symptom of the Church failing to meet the world. Yet, I suspect, in 1961 Guildford was more warmly received than Coventry or Liverpool Metropolitan, but this neither challenges nor inspires. It seems to me to be in line with the Church of England, mid-century: the Church of

Archbishops Lang and Fisher, patrician and remote from the concerns, spiritual or otherwise, of English people. The best thing at Guildford is the sanctuary carpet with its magnificent stag from the name of the hill on which the cathedral stands. In all it may be like the Giants' Causeway in the view of Dr Johnson – worth seeing, but not worth going to see.

Coventry although consecrated only a year after Guildford is from a different generation. Again there was a competition, this time won by Sir Basil Spence; designed in 1951 and completed in 1962. The destruction of the old cathedral apart from the outer walls and the tower and spire gave a spiritual impetus so lacking in Guildford. The decision to set up the altar in the ruins with the cross of charred roof beams and to tell the world this is still Coventry Cathedral was a mark of deep spiritual conviction. Death and resurrection, this is what Christianity is all about.

But is it a modern cathedral? The average English person's idea of modern in many fields remains peculiarly out of date. In architecture the new between-the-wars thinking in Germany made little impact here. To the average Anglican Coventry seemed extraordinarily modern and certainly they would have been much more shocked by some of the other entries. Both bishop and provost had a vision, which *was* a vision and Sir Basil Spence was the man to give them a spiritual building. It began with the conditions drawn up largely by bishop and provost:

> The Cathedral is to speak to us and to generations to come of the Majesty, the Eternity and the Glory of God. God, therefore, direct you. It stands as a witness to the central dogmatic truths of the Christian faith. Architecturally it should seize on those truths and thrust them upon the man who comes in from the street. The cathedral should be built to enshrine the altar. It is the people's altar.[3]

Two important things are recorded by Spence of his first visit in 1950. He recognized that the ruined nave was still a cathedral, and therefore must be preserved. Then he looked north over the space available for the new building and saw 'a great nave and an altar that was an invitation to Communion, and a huge picture behind it. I could not see the altar clearly but through the bodies of the Saints.'[4] That is indeed a vision of a church for the people and a people focussed on the Eucharist, participating in it, but a Church finding its meaning and identity through the Saints.

Spence, with the bishop's support, argued for a central altar but this was refused by the Reconstruction Committee, so the liturgical arrangements are traditional for smallish cathedrals – Chichester, for example – nave, quire, sanctuary. The altar is raised up and almost everyone in the building can see it but even the front row of nave chairs is many feet away. The building is linear, like all cathedrals apart from Liverpool Metropolitan, but it ought to be possible to create a different order on this west-east axis. Could not the high altar be placed at the west end of the raised floor space and the stalls for clergy and choir be placed beyond that?

The huge picture became the Sutherland tapestry, Christ in Majesty. This is the one great masterpiece of Coventry. It isn't an addition – it is essential to the cathedral. One wonders how well it will fare, if like the building itself, it is meant to last for at least five centuries. Michael Sadgrove's book *A Picture of Faith* reveals the spiritual depths of this work and I just comment on the brilliance of its conception and how it rightly dominates the whole cathedral. This is the Christ of Ephesians:

> Measured by God's strength and the might which he exerted in Christ when he raised him from the dead, when he enthroned him at his right hand in the heavenly realms, far above all government and authority, all power and dominion, and any title of sovereignty that can be named, not only in this age but in the age to come. He put everything in subjection beneath his feet and appointed him as supreme head of the church, which is his body and as such holds within it the fullness of him who himself receives the entire fullness of God. (1.19-23)

Spence wrote of the 'jewels in the casket' and of them as things giving 'life and character and make it breathe'. The tapestry is for me the jewel.

Clearly compromises had to be made but Dr Cocke, the architectural historian, writing in the *Church Times* (18 October 1996) denies that these were feeble surrenders and claims that the cathedral has an enduring appeal.

As we move on in time we begin to see the value in things which were not avant-garde when created. We can see the value in things of different styles created at the same time. The problems at Coventry are, however, serious. In addition to those about the position of the altar there are the problems of light. The face of the tapestry is now picked out by a spotlight despite the natural light that comes into the Lady Chapel. That light creates problems for the nave windows, just as the flood of light through the Hutton Screen, which I also think is superb, for the baptistry window. Glass needs to be seen from an interior in which the light comes only through the glass, as for example in King's Chapel, Cambridge, or at its apogee, in Chartres. But Coventry's excellent glass is compromised by the clear light. The nave windows, again difficult to see properly because of the choir stalls, are in themselves very interesting. They are not abstract as an initial look suggests, but full of profound symbolism which can illuminate the struggles of our living. The clear glass though has its point too: the vision of the altar seen through the saints has an importance for the Church as a community formed and shaped by the heroic virtues of the saints, and they gather with us, the whole company of heaven, when we celebrate the Eucharist. The fact that a public footpath goes straight through the huge open porch between the ruins and the new cathedral is important for being a point of access for the man off the street who is to be drawn into the cathedral. The Chapel of Industry too is open to the city with clear glass. It is vital that the Church at worship remembers the world, and actually seeing a bit of it, is a help. Both this chapel and the one for Christian unity have central altars.

Coventry has a unique ministry because of its history. It does speak in the language of the present age. At its heart is the proclamation of the Gospel, the defeat of evil and the triumph of good, the triumph of God's love. Epstein's *St Michael and the Devil* is an eloquent testimony to that.

And so finally, to Portsmouth. This church began as a chapel of ease within the parish of Portsea only ten years after the murder of St Thomas Becket, in whose honour it is dedicated. The original twelfth-century church was heavily damaged in the Civil War of the seventeenth century and the nave and west tower were rebuilt in classical style. Sir Charles Nicholson drew up plans for its enlargement after it became the cathedral of a new diocese, and parts of these were built. The problem was the narrowness of the tower, but opening up the lowest level made it a kind of passage between the old nave, now a quire, and the new nave. The war came putting a stop to this work and the west end was temporarily bricked up. The initiative to continue the building to completion was taken when David Stancliffe became Provost in the 1980s. In between there had been a design for a huge nave, but rebuilding of nearby properties after war damage made that impossible and probably the cost was thought excessive. Michael Drury has now completed the nave and added western turrets which directly complement Nicholson's nave. Nicholson produced designs for several parish church cathedrals, notably at Sheffield where again only part was built. That completion is messy and doesn't make much sense of Sir Charles' work – although given the site that was probably an impossible task. So it is good to see Portsmouth making good use of the Nicholson inspiration. David Stancliffe says that the cathedral invites you to go on a journey. The nave has 'something of an agora or market place. We need to draw people into it, but then challenge them. To step out of the nave, that open airy space, and to go into the dark low tunnel under the tower' takes you into the baptistry, the point of commitment. Beyond that small space lies the old church, which is the quire focussed on both lectern and altar. The bishop's chair is set near the altar, and beyond that elegant classical space lies a fourth – the early medieval chancel. Here in the Chapel of St Thomas is an altar with a wonderful hanging pyx, surmounted by a canopy painted richly. The pyx looks like a great silver egg surrounded by a crown in gold. The journey is from dialogue with the faith, through the waters of baptismal commitment, into the Church where we are fed by word and sacrament, and beyond that to the vision of heaven, seen in the saints and of which the Sacrament reserved, high up, is a sign. The architecture is good: it has grace and beauty, but has little of the complexity, height or exuberance that I have found in greater churches, but this cathedral has become a significant place. Reflecting upon it as I have researched and written this book I see, as I say elsewhere, that this pattern is actually there in many ancient cathedrals. Portsmouth works for me, as Coventry does, because of its spiritual vision: in one the central doctrine of resurrection, in the other the journey of faith. Perhaps other parish church cathedrals, even if they are not able or do not need to build afresh, can explore the spiritual realities in relation to the architecture and find ways of encouraging spiritual renewal.

CHAPTER XXVI

Pride, Cost and Glory

O ne of the things which surprises people about these buildings is how the individuals who created them left their personal mark on them. I do not mean the masons and other artists and craftsmen, although they did in small unobtrusive ways, but the patrons, those who commissioned the buildings. Not content with the records preserved in archives, letters, accounts and so on, they wanted people to see something in the fabric itself. Such a man was James Goldwell. He was Edward IV's Secretary of State and just happened to be in Rome on business when he was appointed to be Bishop of Norwich. He was consecrated in Rome but returned to Norfolk to add to the beauty of his cathedral priory. He reroofed and revaulted the presbytery. This vault has 128 bosses of which no less than ninety-four are of gold wells, a rebus or pun on his name. Furthermore another three, and these among a fairly small number of large bosses, are his coat of arms. That only leaves thirty-one for religious topics, and in fact most of the rest are floral, mainly roses.

Tombs were another way of telling posterity how important you thought you were and many episcopal tombs were commissioned and even completed long before the person died.

All this testifies to the wealth and generosity of these bishops and abbots. All late medieval work is liberally decorated with rebuses, coats of arms, monograms and so on. And this continues today although much more discreetly. A list of corporate benefactors is displayed in Peterborough Cathedral and at Ely the windows of the Lady Chapel bear the names of the companies that sponsored the restoration work.

People want to make their mark and no doubt there was rivalry between neighbouring abbeys and cathedrals as to which could build the best, the highest, the grandest. Many of the finest architectural achievements came from a desire to outdo the work of earlier generations. Rebuildings were certainly done to create something better, more glorious than that which they replaced. A progression of improvement was an essential idea of medieval architecture. And not only then. I'm sure Sir Gilbert Scott thought he could better the medieval splendours when he conceived the huge scale of Liverpool and Sir Edwin Lutyens was attempting to outclass even St Peter's in Rome with his plans for the same city.

For a group of people following an itinerant preacher who had nowhere to lay his head this must seem strange. Jesus did use the synagogues and the Temple but a case can be argued to maintain that we should not have religious buildings at all. That I would not agree is obvious but there are questions about the use of resources and the cost in human terms as well as financial. The lives of ordinary people remained extremely poor whilst so much money and effort was being expended on great churches. But large numbers found work thereby and I don't believe the money would have been distributed to the poor. It rarely is.

We continue to build great churches but usually modestly and with great economy and far more money goes into the preservation of the older buildings. Appeals now tend to be in the £5 million plus bracket and those budgets are minute compared with other projects. A new swimming pool or a concert hall works out at over £40 million and the Millennium Dome, of dubious value, was over £600 million. I reckon the millions spent on repair, restoration and adornment of our greater churches are much better value for money.

Whatever we think about the financial costs, there are human, sometimes spiritual ones as well. The institution of cathedral or abbey has power and one not infrequently feels that the buildings and its music have become idols rather than being the means of grace from God. Recent infightings have done little to show how these Christians love one another. These institutions, where power is held by a few, but also power diversified, seem to have a recipe for conflict built in but it was ever so. The fact that deans and canons are appointed by different sources of authority makes for conflict. Deans and chapters who hold the power presently, and will soon be slightly enlarged into administrative chapters, work in a context where a great many other disempowered people feel extremely involved and it requires great skill to address the issues that arise with sensitivity. However, most chapters function well and I would think as much spleen is vented in PCCs as anywhere else.

Sir William Golding's novel *The Spire* is about the use of power, an overwhelming vision and the dark consequences that can have. Jocelyn, the Dean, has a vision to build a great spire, a vision which is not shared by his fellow priests, but they can't prevent him from starting to build. He says near the beginning of the project, 'I must remember the spire isn't everything' but slowly the spire comes to be exactly that. It sours relationships, and brings disaster in its wake. The first to suffer is the chancellor. 'The services went on and business was done but, as in the burden of some nearly over-whelming weight, the chancellor was removed to his house and an extra terror of senility fell on the older men.' There is a darkness without hope. Jocelyn speaks to the spire: 'I thought you would cost no more than money.' For he begins to see the other costs in damaged human lives, but still the project must go on and the evil grows. Against this Jocelyn becomes more certain of his cause. 'I am about my Father's business,' he declares. Roger, the mason, after the creeping of the earth in the pit beneath the tower, says, 'We've come to the end. That's all there is to it.' His is the voice of reason, or is it cynicism?

Ignoring this the Dean retorts, 'It's a great glory. I see now that it will destroy us of course.' And there's an excitement about it all. No-one had been that high before. Roger asks, 'Have you a machine to measure the weight of the wind? They call it Jocelyn's Folly, don't they?'

'I've heard it called so . . . the folly isn't mine. It's God's Folly. Even in the old days he never asked men to do what was reasonable. Men can do that for themselves. They can buy and sell, heal and govern. But then out of some deep place comes the command to do what makes no sense at all – to build a ship on dry land; to sit among the dunghills; to marry a whore; to set their son on the altar of sacrifice. Then, if men have faith, a new thing comes.'

And there you have it: the folly of divine command or simply overweening human pride. In many places, in many centuries, people have dreamt their dreams and found someone to carry them through. To do what makes no sense at all. That isn't a definition of Christian faith, but to many the great churches, the monastic life, the life of prayer doesn't make much sense. The example of Noah, Job, Hosea and Abraham points us to God's use of what appears to men of the world to be folly and God uses their folly. Doesn't this point to the great example of God's Folly, the Incarnation and the Death and Resurrection of Christ?

Christianity has a logic to it. It is a reasonable faith but in the end it is love that matters, and there's no logic to that. Aren't we glad that Salisbury has its spire rising 400 feet into the sky? Aren't we glad that Ely has its Octagon Tower hanging lightly in space? Aren't we glad for all those other visions of glory? For within the pride and the vision was something of love. Can they not bring inspiration to our

192

generation to dare to do things which make no sense at all, but which contain something fundamental to mankind?

However, let us remember that all human activity comes from mixed motives, and all is touched by the flaws we call sin. Nothing glorious is wrought without cost and the financial part may well be the smaller part. I hope the glory outweighs the cost.

CHAPTER XXVII

A Journey of Spiritual Treasures

In this final chapter I am taking you to several greater churches all over England to share with you some of the things I most enjoyed or found spiritually profitable as I toured the country one spring in preparation for writing this book. We shall go to Liverpool, to Beverley in Yorkshire, to the much-neglected cathedral at Peterborough, to St Alban's, Lincoln, to York, Lichfield, Ely, Oxford, Portsmouth and finally to Devon, to Buckfast.

The north side of Liverpool Cathedral overlooks a deep ravine, so to put a ceremonial porch on that side was strange, but symmetry demanded it. The porch now houses a restaurant, but to the side of it in the western transept is the shop. Most cathedrals have shops of one kind or another and there's nothing special about the shop itself, but above it is a marvellous set of what I call sails. Between a small open circle at the top, and a larger solid one at the bottom hang great curved pieces of cloth. It is like a set of sails flying in regular formation. I find it thrilling. I don't know who created it, or whose idea it was, or even why it is where it is. The white cloth stands out strongly against the deep red of the Wootton stone, and to me is a sign of the Holy Spirit.

Down Hope Street one reaches the Roman Catholic Cathedral. Three things caught my eye here in addition to those I have mentioned elsewhere. Two have to do with the sense of prayerful use that pervades the cathedral. A statue of St Martin of Porres, the Peruvian saint whose life was spent championing the needs of the poor, stands not far from the main entrance. There was a small bunch of flowers left at his feet. That small gesture spoke to me of a living relationship between this seventeenth-century saint and someone in modern Liverpool. The other thing about prayer was the list of services: the daily office and several masses each day, but Evening Prayer is sung on Tuesday and Fridays and in addition the Blessed Sacrament is exposed for two hours in one of the enclosed chapels every day. Somehow this is a more obvious indication that the cathedral is a house of prayer. I was there fairly early in the morning, but there were several people praying and very few just looking around.

The other thing I want to draw your attention to is the arrangement of chapels. I've no idea whether this is deliberate, thought out, or whether just as things have turned out. The original design had a ring of chapels around the circumference of the main space of the cathedral. As the years have passed the uses of these variously shaped spaces have changed. I noticed the connections across the wide space of the cathedral which find their centre in the great solid stone altar. The baptistry is opposite the statue of Abraham by Sean Rice. Both statements of faith and of promise. The patriarch, although old is sent from his home to find a new land. He is promised a son, despite being childless, and told that his descendants will be like the grains of sand on the seashore. And Abraham believes God's promises, he travels to Palestine, and Isaac is born. Christians are the offspring of Abraham. He is our father in the faith. In baptism we start our journey of faith, and God promises us eternal life. Often those promises seem as remote to us as they must have done to Abraham, but he and the Christian community into which we are baptized are signs of God's fulfilment of his promises.

The entrance leads us across the altar to the Blessed Sacrament Chapel. There is again the journey, and the food for the journey, and in the Reserved Sacrament the hope and the mystery of redemption. Jesus says to those who eat his Body and drink his Blood that he will raise them up on the Last Day.

The Chapel is very light. The painting, the glass and the Tabernacle itself are by Ceri Richards in yellow, white and blue. It is the one place inside the cathedral that has no need of artificial light. It draws us across the wide, darkened space, just as Christian hope draws us across the journey of life. The colours speak of delight and joy, of a vibrant life, and the Tabernacle housing the consecrated Host is a reminder of God's hiddenness, the hiddenness of brilliant light, and our need for faith to believe that this simple, ordinary bread actually is the Bread of Life.

From Liverpool across the Pennines and out into the edge of the Yorkshire wolds stands the Minster at Beverley. Two things here to show you. The first just inside the north porch are the sculptures that decorate the string course at the top of the blind arcading of the north aisle. These aren't small, hidden-away carvings. They are sizeable and very much of this world. That a medieval mason was able to put these in such a prominent place, at the right height to be seen and enjoyed says a lot about how our forebears saw life. Nothing is profane for except from sin nothing is beyond the God of creation, and even that

He enfolds in his love. There is humour and satire here. I select a few of these carvings: a coifed woman's head with a lap dog; a bearded man playing a positive organ; a bald bagpipe player; a fox dressed as a bishop in chasuble and crozier; a man who looks like a town crier. They are great fun.

St John of Beverley who, having been Bishop of Hexham and then of York, retired to Beverley which he had founded. He spent the last four years of his life there, dying in 721. He ordained the Venerable Bede who has much to say about him in his History. At the east end of the minster where there ought to be a Lady Chapel there is a display of tapestries made to tell the story of St John. They are simple, direct and have something of the feel of Anglo-Saxon work. Our churches have stories to tell and this one does that rather well.

Beverley was an outpost for the archbishops of York so next let me take you to York. I went just after Easter and was delighted to see a large plain cross of wood hung within the central tower, in front of the coloured organ case. It was draped with a large white cloth. It was a dramatic sight and a vigorous reminder of the reality behind the season of Easter.

That was obviously temporary as I expect might well be a piece of sculpture in St Alban's. The north transept is a chapel for the persecuted, picking up on the story of St Alban. He was a Roman townsman who gave shelter to a Christian priest who was being pursued by the authorities. Alban was so impressed by the prayerful and gentle manner of his guest that when the soldiers came to search the house Alban gave himself up instead of the priest. Then refusing to either betray the priest or to burn incense to the emperor, he was condemned to death. The sculpture is called *Grozny*. This is a city much in the news a few years ago. It lies on the River Terek in the part of Russia that lies between the Black and Caspian Seas. But even if we can't remember the details of Grozny the place exists as it were in many other places: all those communities persecuted by the wars and conflicts of human politics and religion. We think of the old men, the women, the children who are the victims – refugees, often hungry, brutalized by rape and violence, and who seem often to bear the brunt of the inhumanity of the oppressors. The sculpture is made of white plaster of Paris over chicken-wire; so very basic and therefore strong in conviction. It is a kind of pieta. There is a person sitting with the dead body across the lap. The head looks up from the ground. One is struck by this earthed quality – heavily on the ground, but also, low, humbled, beaten. The seated figure has no face, as if his or her

196

humanity has been taken away, and the grief experienced is so harrowing that the arms push us away. This person is beyond our comfort, and it is uncomfortable for us to look. That reminded me of that feeling of intruding on pain and sorrow that I have when the TV cameras invade the privacy of those who are too weak to protect themselves. These images haunt us, and we need them, but I feel it is obscene when the eye of the world focusses in on such hurt and humiliation. Grief requires dignity and I drew away from the sculpture, touched by it, but not being able to stare: those hands drove me away, but at the same time drew me into prayer for all those who suffer the *Grozny* experience. This piece also reminded me that someone mourned over the dead body of Alban. Martyr he certainly was but also loved by friends and neighbours. It is all too easy to forget the reality of the saints' lives and see them only as the coloured images of story books or coloured glass.

St Blaise is a saint of whom little of historical certainty is known. Not that that matters. The stories tell of Blaise healing a boy who was near to death because of a fishbone stuck in his throat, so he has been associated with throat problems, but he is also strongly connected with the wool industry and so is patron of Bradford, and Dubrovnik; the reason being one of the instruments used to torture him. It was like a carding comb used on wool. Now, I'm not sure about any connections between Dubrovnik, an ancient resort on the Dalmatian coast in the former Yugoslavia, and Blaise, but there must be some. A chantry chapel in Lincoln Cathedral for Bishop Russell is dedicated to St Blaise. The wall paintings by Duncan Grant, completed in 1958, are all about the wool industry and the main image is of Christ the Good Shepherd. There are a good many sheep, some of them being sheared, and on the west wall, a harbour scene of Brayford Pool in the lower part of the city. The paintings are effective and strong and I have always liked them, but the chapel now has a small notice reminding us that St Blaise is patron of Dubrovnik and suggesting we pray for the city. Once again, it has been a place like Grozny, an ordinary, historic city just as Lincoln is, torn about by war.

Across the cathedral in the north-east corner of the Angel Quire is the shrine of St Gilbert of Sempringham. Gilbert, like Hugh, is a local saint and it is fitting that this shrine should be here. He created monastic communities for men and women: the women followed the rule of St Benedict and the men that of St Augustine. The shrine consists of several tall, thrown pots for candles and some large bowls filled with sand for votive candles. I remember once going there and a group of boys was sitting on the steps among the pots. One asked if he could put my candle into the sand. Having done this for me he told me I now had to say a prayer. This is one of my treasured spots in the cathedral.

Another is the nave. I find it hard to put into words how I feel about this great space. Fortunately it is often empty of furniture and you can wander slowly around it. Somehow it feels like being inside something that is alive. I can best express my reactions in part of a much longer poem:

Syncopated rhythms march
   nobilmente
   standing tall, drawing out
   goodness,
   as we truly are.

Huge silent spaces splashed
   with vivid purples and
   red-blues
   the arch of melody.

Overwhelming pain of pure beauty,
   grace and crux gloriae
   sea of crystal,
   rainbow protecting
   beasts and elders prostrate
   purging, illuminating
   (beasts in the margin)
   terrible joy.

The pure beauty tears me
   ploughs up the heavy
   clods of humanity
   a seed-bed
   for loving.

That last section probably sums up well the whole subject matter of this book.

I want to give full marks to the Dean and Chapter of Ely for their exhibition – A Glorious Inheritance. The exhibition stands in the south-west transept and it is easy to pass straight by it. For having entered through the Galilee Porch, you come under the western tower and the natural progression is then into the nave, but a notice suggests that you might want to discover more about the faith which this building expresses. I have no idea how many of Ely's visitors actually go and look, but for those who do, and they will be folk who want to know more, then there is an excellent presentation. Not only is it very well displayed but by using sculptures, glass, misericords, photos of people and activities in and around the cathedral it shows how this particular place and these particular people, down the centuries, have lived out and do live out the Christian faith. It isn't easy to encompass the beliefs of Christians in a relatively brief display, but Ely has made an excellent shot at it. And when you reach the shop you discover you can buy a copy of it to take away and mull over.

On the whole these greater churches assume their visitors know about the faith. I think this is probably a mistake, and to use the building to illustrate the faith helps visitors to see how the church grows out of the beliefs of the community which built it and continue to worship in it. In some places many of the visitors are from the Far East. Now, one shouldn't assume that no Japanese are Christians but I have no doubt from the way they behave that the majority of these visitors have very little idea of what Christianity is about – and that will also be true of many Westerners who are simply doing the culture tour. The problem is how do you convey the essentials of belief without being naive and over simplistic. Notices attached to altars, lecterns or whatever, explaining the belief behind them rarely work, but an exhibition like that at Ely is a great step forward.

In Cheshire, at Norton Priory, there is a museum with good displays but the thing that pleased me most was a leaflet called 'God's Call' – spiritual life then and now. It consists of a nun's response to the question 'What do you love most about the life you have chosen?' It is one of those extremely rare things, especially at a ruined site, to remind people that the Church and monasteries still exist.

Hans Feibusch was one of the great artists of the twentieth century. Principally he was a painter of murals and there are many churches and other public buildings with examples of his work. But in his later years he lost much of his sight, and then he turned to sculpture. One of his pieces, commissioned by Peter Walker, the then Bishop of Ely, stands in the space of the western tower there. It is a welcoming Christ: simple, majestic, drawing the observer in. This is also true of the Christ in Majesty by Peter Ball above the Octagon Pulpit. It is a tall figure with long feet and fingers: wood but decorated with metallic paints in gold and bronze. The hands, one raised in blessing, show the wounds. The crucifix above most pulpits are bland and insignificant, but this was has grandeur, majesty and pulls you towards it. This is the attractive Christ who gently but inexorably draws all to himself. Two more touches which make the Ely experience good.

Now we move from fenland city to university city, from a cathedral which dominates the landscape to one hidden away. Finding Oxford Cathedral which is also the Chapel of Christ Church is not easy, but you find yourself approaching it via a small cloister. Architecturally this is nothing distinguished, but I was delighted to see it wild. Amid the smooth, creamy gold Cotswold stone and amid the splendour and civilizing atmosphere of this very man-made place, where even the gardens tend to be formal, here is a bit of wilderness: daisies, buttercups, forget-me-nots, cowslips growing amid the long grasses. That is a small space to lift the heart partly because it is so unexpected but also because to me it says that underneath the urbanity of Oxford, lies a beating heart of human passions. If we can take something of that reality with us into the cathedral it will give a sharper edge to what we discover. Frideswide's monastery would have known these wild flowers. We treat them as weeds because of their profusion, but our carelessness or thoughtlessness has driven many such flowers near to extinction. Our towns and cities like so much of ourselves are products of having driven the natural away: stone pavements instead of grassy paths, parks with smooth lawns rather than fields, fountains driven by electricity (however wonderful) instead of natural waterfalls. I'm not urging us back to some rural idyll, which never existed, but just asking for a bit of natural freshness amid the necessary artificiality of the city.

And so back across the middle of England to Peterborough. The fan-vaulted retroquire is often a place of storage for chairs, and so I had some difficulty in seeing one of the two sculptures there: *Our Lady of Lamentation* to the south, and *St Peter*, to the north. He was hemmed in with chairs. *Our Lady* is of creamy-white Beer stone, *St Peter* of oak. The one by Polly Verity, the other the work of Simon Latham. Mary is tall, thin, holding her baby. Her left hand is under his thigh and one of his hands grasps her veil. Mary is holding his other hand. Most mothers and child express the lowliness, the love, the humility and joy of Our Lady. More rarely we see images of her by the Cross, but the two come together here. Simeon having held the Christ Child in the Temple says to Mary: This child is destined to be a sign that will be rejected; and you too will be pierced to the heart (Luke 2.34). Any mother feels delight and joy in her child, but more than a few moments' thought of what the future holds reveal the pain and hurt that the child will endure, and indeed cause. Mary knows her Son will share that endurance and perhaps in her wisdom she begins to perceive even as she holds him, small and vulnerable in her arms, that the man he will grow into will hold all the pain of the world, and for this she laments. This is the vague possibility that finds its full, heavy burden in the pietas. Polly Verity catches a lot of this.

St Peter is young, tough, boyish. The piece was made when Simon Latham was artist in residence at the Cathedral in 1991. The 'caption' quotes St Matthew: Peter called to him: 'Lord, if it is you, tell me to come to you over the water.' 'Come,' said Jesus. Peter got down out of the boat, and walked over the water towards Jesus (14.28-9). Peter is the impulsive man of faith, who makes bold starts and then runs away. Later, you recall, he said he would stand by Jesus, even die with him, but then runs away from Gethsemane and denies he even knows Jesus. And there is that later legend of Peter as bishop in Rome who, under persecution, is fleeing. He meets Jesus and Peter asks him where he is going. Jesus says that he is going into the city to be crucified again. Peter has to return and face the consequences of his faith – even if that means martyrdom. I'm not sure this carving is about all that; but it shows the keen young man, actually larger than life. A muscular figure sitting on an edge but about to cast himself off onto the water. There are splits in the wood which to me say something about the flawed nature of humanity. This Peter is about to risk his faith. Will the water hold him up? We perhaps see ourselves in him, but do we have the staying power? Will we risk our faith? Can we actually get as far as Jesus across the water, or will we, like Peter, see the power of the waves and find ourselves sinking beneath them?

I could go on with many more things that delight me in our greater churches, for I have said nothing about the buildings themselves, apart from Lincoln's nave, nothing about the glass, although I suspect the rest of the book reveals much of those things that inspire, provoke, strengthen, humble and bring me closer to God.

I come finally to Devon and the real Abbey Church of Buckfast. Real because it is the Church of a living Benedictine community. There are a good many Benedictine houses in England, some very small, others as large as those of the Middle Ages. Few have greater churches, although the pattern can be seen in others. Buckfast was a monastery founded in 1018 but like all the others dissolved under Henry VIII. However, the site became available in the late nineteenth century and Benedictine monks returned. The church was rebuilt between 1907 and 1937. Only one monk survives from those days – Brother Paschal. The monks learnt the skills they needed – bricklaying, scaffolding, plastering, stonecutting and glazing – just as it is possible some of their medieval forebears had. It was always said that Cistercian monks built their own buildings, but not often believed. Buckfast shows it can be done. It is not a huge building but it is a greater church: three-storeyed, vaulted with many spaces, quire, nave, chapels. And, like the cathedrals and other greater churches in this book, but unlike most abbeys, it is much visited – something like 500,000 every year. It would be interesting to know if their visitors are different in kind from the normal cathedral visitors. The abbot in an interview in *Country Living*, December 1997, says that although a great many tell him how inspiring the place is, they nearly always add on something about the fact that they are not really religious or anything. This a community forty-plus strong and with a budget of £1 million a year. Now, the average cathedral staff will probably be larger than that, although many are part-time and/or volunteers, and the turnover may be several millions per year, but I do think Buckfast can teach a great deal to those who are responsible for our greater churches. The Rule of St Benedict is kept well in a modern monastery and the guests come as Benedict says they will. The community has to earn its living, just as the early communities did. Rents and tithes give way to income from shops, stained glass, pottery, vestments, retreatants, gifts, legacies, but the essence is the same. Brother Paschal, who as been at Buckfast for over seventy years, says he has enjoyed everything he has done. After years on the building, he spent thirty years caring for the bees, with the world-famous Brother Adam; then twenty years in the kitchen. Now he engages in housework. You have to be willing, despite your inclinations, to offer your talents in perhaps unexpected ways for the good of the monastic life. And that centres around the Office and Mass day by day, as it ever did.

'Nothing is to be preferred to the love of Christ,' wrote Benedict (RB 72.11). If our greater churches are to survive as beacons of Christian faith they must be places where nothing, not the building itself, not the income, not the tourists, nothing comes before the love of Christ. There must be no compromise. First, last, and in between these are churches – nothing else, and if they are not, they are nothing.

Notes

Introduction
1. Glyn Coppack's *Abbeys and Priories*. B.T. Batsford and English Heritage has plans of St Augustine's Abbey, Canterbury on pages 33 and 40.

I. Spirituality
1. The quotation from Robert Waddington I have failed to trace.
2. The Rule of St Benedict is available in several editions. I have used one translated by David Parry, OSB, published by DLT, 1984.
3. The quotation from Thomas Maude comes from *Guided by a Stonemason*, I.B. Taurus, 1997.
4. The quotation from Richard Holloway is from *Crossfire*, Collins, 1988.
5. Rose Tremain, *Sacred Country*, p. 130.
6. 'A place of daring' comes from Sir William Golding's book *The Spire*, Faber and Faber, 1964, p. 44.

II. Bezalel and Aholiab
1. T.S. Eliot's lecture was published by the Friends of Chichester Cathedral as 'The Value and Use of Cathedrals in England Today', 1951.
2. R. Somerset Ward's book is *To Jerusalem*, Mowbray-Morehouse Publishing, 1994, quotations on pages 161 and 164.
3. The Yeats poem is pp. 255f in the Papermac edition, 1989.
4. Marion J. Hatchett's book is *Sanctifying Life, Time and Space*, Seabury Press, New York, 1976. The reference is to chapter I.
5. The Auden is on p. 238 of *Collected Shorter Poems*, Faber.
6. Iris Murdoch, *The Bell*, Penguin edition, pp. 190-1.
7. The Paul Binding quotation comes from a memoir of David Cecil published by Dovecote Press in 1990, p. 142.

III. Stone
1. Throughout this chapter I am indebted to Thomas Maude. The

quotations are from pages 81 and 88 of his book. Also, as anyone who has read them will know, I am indebted to the sermons of Michael Stancliffe and especially 'What Mean These Stones?' That comes in a book called *Jacob's Ladder*, SPCK, 1987.

2. The hymn verse is from J.M. Neale's translation of Blessed City in the New English Hymnal 204. It is verse 4.

IV. Glass

1. The phrase 'a trailer for paradise' is from Edward Heathcote in *Church Building* issue 42, 1996, p. 70.
2. John Hayward's window was featured in several *Church Building* issues: 20, 33 and 49 of 1991/92, 1995 and 1998 respectively. The reference is to the last of these – page 57.

V. Facades and Porches

1. The Jim Cotter quotation is from *Yes . . . Minister?* p. 44, Cairns Publications, Sheffield, 1992.

VI. The Nave

1. 'Heritage and Renewal' was published by Church House Publishing in 1994, page 12.
2. Michael Perhams's comments are in *900 Years* published by Jarrold Publishing, Norwich in 1996, a book edited by Jim Wilson.
3. J.G. Davies's book *The Secular Use of Church Buildings*, SCM Press, 1968 was very helpful in preparing this chapter.

VII. Crucifixion and Resurrection

1. Pamela Tudor-Craig's comment is from 'The Image of Christ Crucified', p. 35 in *Church Building* issue 12, 1989.
2. Dom Philip Jebb's remarks are in *A Touch of God*, edited by Maria Boulding, SPCK, 1982, p. 12.
3. Paul Iles' introduction to a leaflet published at Hereford called 'The Hereford Corona', p. 2, 1992.

VIII. The Quire

1. Alan Wicks' words are from an article in *Church Music*, R.S.C.M., 1988, p. 11.

IX. A House for an Altar

1. R.N. Swanson, *Catholic England*, Manchester University Press, 1993.
2. Otter Memorial Paper Number 7: *Chichester Tapestries*, pp. 25f. The quotation is on page 29.

X. Extensions for Saints

1. Tim Tatton-Brown, *Great Cathedrals of Britain*, BBC, 1989, pp. 75f.
2. 'People Look East' is in the *Oxford Book of Carols*, 133, OUP, 1928.
3. David Stancliffe wrote about Portsmouth in *Church Building* issue 20, 1991/92, p. 27.
4. 'Lumen Gentium', 49, Vatican Council II, Austin Flannery DP (ed.), Dublin, 1975, cf. 1 Timothy 2, 5.
5. 'return to our places' is a reference to Eliot's poem 'The Journey of the Magi', *Collected Poems 1909-62*, Faber, 1963, p. 110.
6. Sir Nikolaus Pevsner and Priscilla Metcalf, *The Cathedrals of England*, 2 volumes (1. Southern England; 2. Midland, Eastern and Northern England), Viking Penguin, 1985. These collect together the entries on cathedrals from the Buildings of England Series. Below I just refer to them as Pevsner. This first quotation is p. 315 in 1.

XI. Pilgrimage

1. Stephen Platten's phrase comes on p. 20 of his *Pilgrims*, Fount, 1996.
2. Eliot, 'Journey of the Magi', p. 109 of *Collected Poems*, 1963.

XII. Death, Burial, Chantries

1. Dorothy L. Sayers' translation and commentary is published by Penguin, 1955. This is to be found on page 58 of volume 2.
2. Christopher Daniel; *Death and Burial in Medieval England*, Routledge, 1997, p. 2.
3. Clarke, *Liturgy and Worship*, 1932, p. 22.

XIII. Community

1. ARCIC stands for the Anglican Roman Catholic International Commission. It was established by Pope Paul VI and Archbishop Michael Ramsey, and recently re-affirmed by Pope John Paul II and the present Archbishop of Canterbury. It has published many reports (SPCK/CTS) since 1971.
2. Annie Dillard's book is: *Pilgrim at Tinker's Creek*, p. 5.
3. *The Rule of St Augustine* is published by DLT 1996.
4. The Dean of Bristol in his installation sermon: published by the Friends of Bristol Cathedral Report 1998, p. 49.
5. June Osborne in *Church Building* issue 51, May 1998.
6. Eliot, 'The Rock', p. 168 of *Collected Poems*, 1963.
7. Richard Giles, *Re-pitching the Tent*, Canterbury Press, Norwich, p. 87.

XV. Precincts
1. *Minster Yard* by Kathleen Major, Lincoln Minster Pamphlets, 2nd series, no 7, 1974, p. 11.

XVI. Kings and Queens
1. Tatton-Brown summary on p. 43.

XVII. Episcopal
1. Gabriel Hebert, *Liturgy and Society*, Faber, 1935. He writes about episcopacy on pp. 155-8.
2. ARCIC Report 1981, CTS/SPCK, 1982, pp. 54f.
3. Tim Tatton-Brown p. 37.

XVIII. Pre-1066 and Romanesque
1. Tim Tatton-Brown has details of the archaeology, pp. 19f.

XIX. Cistercians
1. Otto von Simpson, *The Gothic Cathedral*, Princeton, 3rd edition, 1988.
2. Zarnecki, *The Monastic Achievement*, Thanks and Hudson, 1972, the quotation is on p. 74.
3. Dom David Knowles, *The Monastic Order in England*, CUP, 1940, vol i, p. 20.
4. An undated pamphlet.

XX. Gothic
1. Otto von Simpson, *The Gothic Cathedral, Princeton*, 3rd edition, p. 51.
2. Eliot, p. 184.
3. H. Daniel-Rops, *Cathedral & Crusades*, London, 1957, p. 366.

XXII. Reformation
1. Dom David Knowles, *The Monastic Order*, vol iii, CUP from 1940, p. 146.
2. Crowland is featured in *Church Building*, Summer 1986.
3. Elizabeth Ruth Obbard, *The History and Spirituality of Walsingham*, Canterbury Press, Norwich, 1995, pp. 83-4.

XXIII. St Paul's Cathderal
1. Pevsner 1, p. 133.

XXIV. The Eighteenth and Nineteenth Centuries

1. Alec Clifton-Taylor, *The Cathedrals of England*, Thames and Hudson, p. 235.
2. Pevsner Vol 2, p. 171.
3. Pevsner Vol 2, p. 51.
4. Pevsner Vol 2, p. 51.

XXV. The Nineteenth and Twentieth Centuries

1. Gabriel Hebert, esp pp. 126-7, 129 and 143-4 for the three quotations.
2. The diocese of St Emundsbury and Ipswich was formed out of two archdeaconries, one in Norwich diocese and the other in Ely, and so both titles were retained for the new diocese. The cathedral is in Bury St Edmunds.
3. Sir Basil Spence, *Phoenix at Coventry*, Collins, 1962, pp. 15-16.
4. Ibid., p. 18.